HOW TO INFLUENCE YOUR KIDS FOR GOOD

HOW TO INFLUENCE YOUR KIDS FOR GOOD

SARA DIMERMAN, PSYCHOLOGIST

Collins

How to Influence Your Kids for Good

Published by Collins, an imprint of HarperCollins Publishers Ltd.

Originally published by John Wiley & Sons Ltd under the title
Character Is the Key: 2009
First published by HarperCollins Publishers Ltd under the title
Character Is the Key in an ebook edition: 2013
This Collins paperback edition: 2015

HarperCollins books may be purchased for educational, business, or sales promotional use through our Special Markets Department.

HarperCollins Publishers Ltd
2 Bloor Street East, 20th Floor
Toronto, Ontario, Canada M4W 1A8

www.harpercollins.ca

Library and Archives Canada Cataloguing in Publication information is available upon request.

ISBN 978-1-44344-222-0

Printed and bound in the United States of America
RRD 9 8 7 6 5 4 3 2 1

In loving memory of my mom.
Your goodness lives on . . .
in me, my children, and my children's children.

To my children, Talia and Chloe,
without whom I wouldn't be as passionate
about writing parenting books.

Contents

Introduction 1

Part One

Chapter 1 – Taking a Stand: Defining and Modelling Your Core Values 21

Chapter 2 – Life's Lessons: Learning by Observing 35

Chapter 3 – Parenting Today for Tomorrow 41

Chapter 4 – Modelling as They Grow: From Tots to Teens 51

Chapter 5 – Handling Conflict with Your Co-Parent (Even after Divorce) 59

Chapter 6 – Teaming Up with Your Kids 69

Chapter 7 – Joining Forces with Educators 79

Part Two

Chapter 8 – Family as a Foundation 93

Chapter 9 – The Family Plan 103

Chapter 10 – Feedback from Families 133

Part Three

Chapter 11 – Putting the Pieces Together: One Character Attribute at a Time 149

Chapter 12 – Focus on Empathy 155

Chapter 13 – Focus on Fairness 165

Chapter 14 – Focus on Courage 171

Chapter 15 – Focus on Honesty 177

Chapter 16 – Focus on Initiative 189

Chapter 17 – Focus on Integrity 195

Chapter 18 – Focus on Optimism 201

Chapter 19 – Focus on Perseverance 207

Chapter 20 – Focus on Respect 213
Chapter 21 – Focus on Responsibility 221

Conclusion 227
Acknowledgments 231
References 235
Index 239

If truth, honour and integrity
Live in heavens high
I thank you for your example
And for helping me reach to the sky

If kindness and compassion
If knowing right from wrong
Have their place in music
Then you are both my song

If sustenance, warmth and comfort,
Happiness, laughter and fun
Help a seed to flourish and grow
Then you are the rays of my sun

If passion and vitality
Are colours bright and bold
Then you are both my rainbow,
My silver and my gold

If feelings from the heart
Expression and emotion
Are the endless waters of the sea
Then you are both my ocean

If to feel excited
To hope and to aspire
Is a burning flame inside my soul
Then you are both my fire

If unconditional love and support
Is the branch of a tree up high
I'm the longest tallest tree in the world
With my branches in the sky

Thank you for who I am
Thank you for who I will be
If it weren't for both of you
Then I would not be me

—written by a bride to her parents

Introduction

"Modelling isn't one way of influencing people. It's the only way."
—Albert Einstein

There's no rehearsing being a parent. We're just thrown on stage, without a lot of training. There's no pre-written script, no lines to memorize. And each child is different, so it's hard to see how there *could be* a script that would cover them all. That's what makes being a parent so challenging. Parenting requires a lot of improvisation—being able to pick up on cues and read between the lines.

So we make it up as we go along, hoping for a happy ending.

We do the best we can. But it's a hectic world and many of us are spread pretty thin, trying to parent and earn a living at the same time. And there seem to be a thousand influences on our children that are not easy for us to control, from school to play to TV and movies to the internet and electronic games.

Then we look around one day and our children are not acting like the kind of people we hoped they would be. They're displaying all sorts of behaviours that we don't like and never wanted. And it seems very hard to turn things around.

Most parents that come to see me are pretty exhausted. They've run out of ideas to bring about change. They're tired of having to offer rewards for good behaviour. They want their children to co-operate because they care. They find themselves in a tug of war for power—they ask their children to do something and are faced with "Make me!"

If you're like these parents, you may be feeling hopeless, helpless, or on the road to giving up. Let's run down some of the common problems that you may be seeing in your children:

- not fulfilling everyday responsibilities like getting up for school on time, doing homework, cleaning bedrooms, and other chores
- not following the family's rules: breaking curfews, climbing out of windows after being told to stay home, sneaking onto the computer after they have been asked not to, pretending to go to school and then spending the day at the mall with a friend
- not wanting to spend time together as a family
- calling their parents ugly names, or expressing hate for them
- when out in public, showing bad manners; having no consideration for adults or younger children who may be with them in an enclosed space such as an elevator or a bus shelter
- being mean to other kids (including siblings) or to small animals; taunting or teasing others mercilessly; acting violently in and out of school
- being lazy: wanting to get the most goodies for the least effort
- lack of patience and perseverance, short attention spans, giving up too easily on a task
- behaving with a sense of entitlement, as if the world owes them something
- being overly influenced by others: being coerced into behaviours like drinking, smoking, and promiscuity because of peer group pressure.

Faced with this litany of misbehaviour, what you may be wishing is that your children would act like different people. That they would have an inner compass that would guide them to make better choices, and would motivate them to meet you halfway, acting more like you were all on the same team.

You may also wish your own performance could be better. When asked to critique themselves, many parents tend to say that they don't *want* to be constantly nagging and yelling and getting angry, and they wish they could act more like their true selves. "The person I show to my kids isn't really me," one parent recently told me. "I lose patience with my kids and get frustrated. I say things I don't mean and fight for rules even *I* don't think are fair, just to win. I'm a *better person* than that."

There's a simple way of summing all this up: it's all about *character*. We wish that our children (and ourselves) would do a better job of demonstrating good character. There are various traits that we think of as being part of that, like integrity and honesty and consideration for others. We feel that if our children could somehow get an injection of good character, a lot of the practical details would take care of themselves. A teen with more integrity would remain more true to herself, and not feel the compulsion to drink alcohol or use drugs just because "other kids do." A child who was more honest would not lie about whether he was going to school. Children with more consideration for others would be less likely to tease, taunt, and be mean.

It's a worthy goal: to instil better character in our children. Is there a way to do it—to influence our children to become persons of character?*

Yes, there is, and the clue to it lies in another thing that parents often report to me. They say that they find themselves imitating

* One can speak of good character or bad character. When I use the word "character" in this book without qualifying it (as in "persons of character"), I mean good character.

the very things their own parents did, often not to good effect. One mother reported to me, "I swear I'll never borrow from my own parents' tired old lines or scream as loudly as they did, but then I do, without intending to. It's as if their words are recorded in my brain and played back through my own lips. I hear their voices echo through me, like I've become them."

This simple fact—that we tend to imitate our own parents' behaviour—turns out to be the guidepost we need. It points to a major key to successful parenting that is the central pillar of this book, and a growing international movement. That key is called *modelling character,* and it simply means showing your children what kind of person they should be, by *being* that kind of person yourself. We will talk about many ways of instilling or fostering good character traits, but the most basic and powerful method of them all, without which the others won't work, is to lead by example—to demonstrate those traits yourself, in a way that communicates their value to your children. More briefly, it's about letting your kids see what it means to be a good person.

As parents, we are role models by default. We don't have a choice. No special training, talent, or thought is demanded of us. It just happens. Children, on both a conscious and unconscious level, absorb everything we say and do, and then imitate our example—good and bad. Most kids won't admit to this. They'll say things like, "I never want to smoke; it's gross and makes your fingers yellow." Then, at the age of 12, they'll sneak a cigarette out of your pack and smoke it behind your house with a friend.

Ever overheard or watched your child playing house or dress-up with a friend or sibling? Like a mirror, you'll see yourself reflected in his or her words and actions. When they're four and mimicking our bad behaviour, we laugh and call it cute. When they're 14, it's no longer a laughing matter.

Some of what children learn to imitate is no surprise. Children will swear if they hear us swear. They will show us disrespect if we spend most of our time yelling and screaming at them. They will be impatient and intolerant if we always make them hurry and yell when they accidentally spill their drink. Children practise what they see, *much* more than what we preach.

But a lot of what children learn from us is not so obvious. A mom and dad came to see me about how to deal with sibling rivalry in their home. Their two daughters, aged seven and four, fought constantly with each other. The parents were at the end of their rope in dealing with the friction, and were looking for help in understanding why the girls could not get along. After asking them about each child in great detail, I told the parents that it seemed that their seven-year-old, on her own, was quite easy-going and even-tempered. However, she seemed triggered by her rambunctious younger sister. The parents admitted that they too had a difficult time coping with their younger child, that she purposely went against their requests not to do something, and that she was destructive and created chaos out of calmness. The dad said that he especially had a hard time with his four-year-old when he was trying to work out of his home office in the evening—she purposely pulled papers off his desk and would not stop or leave when asked to.

I asked, "What do you do when you're feeling angry or frustrated with her?" The mom looked over at her husband and laughed. He looked back at her and blushed. He tried telling me what he thought I would want to hear, but his wife gently steered him back to the truth. He admitted that he usually screamed at her and called for his wife to "come take her away." At some point, both parents recognized the connection between the dad's actions and his older daughter's behaviour towards the youngest member of the family. Until that moment, neither parent had considered how the dad's response to frustration was being echoed by his seven-year-old, nor how important it was for him to model alternative ways to respond to her behaviour and behave when frustrated or angry. Over time, once the dad had made some improvements in his response towards his younger child, the parents noticed a significant change in the way that their seven-year-old responded to her too.

Some of what our children learn from us is more indirect, but just as potent. For example, whether or not you show responsibility by arriving at your child's school on time, whether you show empathy by not sending snacks to school that may have come into contact with nuts, and whether you treat your own parents—their grandparents—with respect and care, are all examples of modelling character, either positively or negatively.

So the question isn't "Are you going to model for your kids?" You're modelling now; you have in the past; and you will in the future. The question is "*What* are you going to model?" If you take a closer look at what your children are doing and saying—both at play and while interacting with you—and you're not happy with what you're seeing and hearing, this is your cue that it's time to start behaving differently to bring about change in the way they behave.

In this book I will explore in detail what traits are thought to make up good character—the ten chosen by educators as most important—and present a step-by-step plan for first deciding which characteristics you most want your children to gain, then how to influence by modelling them in a conscious, deliberate, and authentic way. Modelling is the core, but there's more, and along the way I will talk about other ways of encouraging, teaching, and reinforcing good character in your kids, your family, and yourself.

The first step in learning to model character more effectively is to take a hard look at what is going on now in your family. It means observing your children's behaviour, reflecting on your own behaviour, and recognizing the connection between the two. You will become aware of the "unconscious" modelling you've been doing, some of which hasn't realized the results you wanted. It takes courage to do this, a willingness to be open-minded and self-critical. But the potential rewards are immense. When you decide to take conscious control over this area and deliberately model character traits that you have carefully chosen, then observe the effect of this on your children, you become empowered in an amazing new way. What used to be semi-instinctive now becomes a conscious, planned activity, and what used to be hit and miss takes on a sure aim.

This process of taking control over what used to be a haphazard process and turning it into a systematic plan, I will refer to as "modelling with intention," where "intention" means purpose or planning.

At this point I would like to step back and give you the context for what I've covered so far, by telling you more about who I am and where this book came from.

A Little Background

About Myself

I'm a psychologist, registered with the College of Psychologists of Ontario, and I'm married and a parent of two daughters, aged 16 and 23. I've been counselling parents, individuals, couples, and families for 25 years, while offering expert advice to the media and writing articles and books.

In 1990, I founded the Parent Education Resource Centre in Thornhill, Ontario. I did this out of the belief that as parents, we have the power to influence our children for good, and to turn difficult situations at home into more manageable situations even when we don't think we can. Time and again, I have observed that the apple doesn't fall far from the tree and that children copy their parents' behaviour. Therefore, I have always been an advocate of parents modelling character and encourage parents to *show and share*—to *show* what they want to see in their children and to explicitly *share* what it is they are doing.

About Character Education

Schools have been addressing values all along, but the way has not always been smooth—especially in the last half century. Since ancient times, people have believed that part of what children should learn at school is good character, including what moral values apply in life. It was easier to inculcate values in times when there was broad agreement across society about what was right and wrong and how children should behave. As society became more culturally diverse and more secularized, it became less clear exactly how to teach values in schools—and *whose values* should be taught.[1] An educational philosophy called "values clarification"[2] was tried—which recommended that teachers help students "clarify" their own self-chosen values—but it seemed to raise more questions than it solved. What was needed was a way to instil solid, universal *principles* in children without getting embroiled in specific moral disputes (some of them the "hot-button" issues of the day) and without getting into the dogmas of specific organized religions.

The *Character Matters* program was initiated by the school board in my district in the early 2000s. Dr. Avis Glaze, then Associate Director of Education for the York Region District School Board, and John Havercroft, Superintendent of Schools for the same board, also realized the increasing need for an intentional approach to character education. The Columbine school tragedy and other incidents of school violence, local and international, were a wake-up call to educators that a problem they were already aware of—the general decline in values among students—had now gone too far. Violence and bullying were among the symptoms, but there were many other problem behaviours, and the root cause was a decline in children learning what it means to be a good person. Glaze and her team put a proposal together and approached school trustees about starting a character development program in York Region schools.

Community meetings followed, and the program received an overwhelmingly positive response. Participants listed about 60 potential attributes and then narrowed them down to those most worthy of being modelled and taught. In the end, they unanimously agreed on ten—**respect, responsibility, honesty, empathy, fairness, initiative, courage, perseverance, optimism, and integrity**. These are general principles or "virtues" on which most people can agree, but in their simplicity, they are also extremely powerful. If modelled and taught effectively, they can bring about huge change for the better in children's behaviour. And as we'll see in Chapter 1, the process entails adopting broad principles, after which families are free to work out answers to more specific moral issues in their own unique ways. When a child believes, for example, in responsibility, honesty, integrity, and respect, it is much easier for a family to work out their own guidelines on issues such as swearing, pre-marital sex, and the amount and content of TV and electronic games.

As the York Region's District School Board's website explains, character education is not a separate class, but rather is woven into the cross-section of school life. "An English teacher may pay special attention to the character traits of a character in a novel or may point out such attributes as initiative, empathy and fairness in a poem. A math teacher may stress the perseverance of those students who have worked hard to improve. A science teacher may stress the importance of being responsible as a member of a lab group."

After the program was introduced in schools, it had positive effects not only in class but beyond, in school-wide anti-bullying and peer-conflict mediation programs, for example. The wider community, too, flourished as character was consciously incorporated into businesses and the arts: I see notices in the local newspaper announcing Character Awards evenings to acknowledge the way in which local businesses, organizations, and individuals have modelled the characteristics consistent with being a community of character.

But still, there was something missing. My epiphany came when I attended a character assembly at my daughter Chloe's school. I watched proudly as she (then seven years old) walked to the front of the gymnasium to accept that month's character award, for showing respect. And then it occurred to me: this is great, but what about the parents who *aren't* here today? How can we bring this into homes so that parents can make the contribution that only they are capable of making?

And so the idea for this book was born.

There's a kind of war for children's souls going on. We're all aware that many influences in children's lives are negative, not the least of which is what I call the world of "screens": TV, movies, computers, the internet, and video games. As educator Dr. Marvin Berkowitz* says, the popular media make it "a heck of a lot harder to raise children. First, the sheer dosage of it. Secondly, the horribly graphic nature of what they are exposed to and thirdly, how ambiguous it is. It's often hard to tell the good and bad guys apart."[3] He mentions Tony Soprano, the killer we root for, and Dexter, the psychopath who is seen as a hero. On top of these external influences, there have been changes in the family (some related to the need for both parents to work) that have also left children more exposed.

The good news is that the cavalry has arrived, in the form of a widespread realization that an old-fashioned-sounding thing called "character" really matters, and if we don't take active measures to shape children's characters, they may just be shaped for us, and not in the ways we would want. Today, the movement to model, teach, and otherwise build good character is international, vibrant, and steadily growing. It is a great time

* Dr. Berkowitz is McDonnell Professor of Character Education and Co-Director of the Center for Character and Citizenship at the University of Missouri-St. Louis.

for parents to get on board, because they have so many allies, and this book will tell you how.

I have centred the book on the ten attributes mentioned earlier. I will define them with concrete examples, as well as offer you many ideas on how to teach, influence, and intentionally model them to your children. And you will likely come up with additional positive attributes that you want to work on along the way.

How This Book Works

How to Influence Your Kids for Good is organized into three sections.

If we picture our quest as a sort of voyage, Part One is the preparation for launch, including outfitting and fuelling, and an initial spin near the harbour. It will lay out the primary tools you'll need for building character in your children, empower you with the realization that with these tools you can take your family to a better place, and get you started on modelling for your children.

Chapter 1 is about defining the core beliefs and values that you want to focus on for your family. I'll invite you to rank the attributes of good character, and to compare notes on this with your partner. I'll also suggest some interesting moral situations that parents and children may face; mulling them over will help you calibrate your moral compass. Then I'll give pointers so you can start modelling more consciously as soon as you feel ready. In Chapter 2 I'll talk about learning (and teaching) from others' actions and how you can turn even poor examples into teachable moments. Chapter 3 will focus on how to keep tomorrow in mind as a parent, rather than limiting your view to what makes today easier. If your decisions are keyed to your kids' long-term character, they'll be better decisions. Chapter 4 will explore the various stages in a child's life and how your modelling of character can be tailored to each. Finally, Chapters 5 to 7 will talk about the huge advantages to be gained by partnering with your co-parent (even after a divorce), with your children, and with your children's teachers, in your effort to build character in your kids.

Part Two of *How to Influence Your Kids for Good* will get you and your family, as a full-fledged team, well and truly launched on the character-building voyage. Chapter 8 starts with a discussion of how to achieve more time together as a family, and then moves on to the crucial how-to's of conducting an effective family meeting. Then Chapter 9, the heart of the book, presents what I call The Family Plan: a detailed, step-by-step guide to the crucial first family meetings, with worksheets to help you navigate. I also provide definitions and examples of the ten key attributes belonging to a "good" person that you can share and discuss with your spouse and children. At the end of the four-week process, you will be on your way towards the future you want as a family.

Before you actually begin the program detailed in Chapter 9, I suggest that you read through it and Chapter 10, where you'll get real-life feedback from families who have been through the process you're about to begin. That will give you a good idea of what to expect and will brace you with a sense that this *can* be done.

If your spouse hates to read (and you're tired of highlighting the "important" parts), or if you need a refresher, you'll appreciate the "Short & Sweet" section at the end of most chapters in this book. In these sections, I'll sum up what's been covered in that chapter.

Part Three of the book (Chapters 11 to 22) introduces you to the once-a-month meeting and describes some important spots to visit during the first ten months of the voyage, devoting a short chapter to each of the ten crucial characteristics that influence "good" behaviour. Your entire family is encouraged to focus on each of these attributes, one per month, so that everyone has a chance to fully experience and understand them. Each chapter also offers a fun exercise that the family can do together, to stimulate understanding and discussion on everyone's part. The exercises were created by Dynamix, a Canadian-based organization that is a leader in team-building and character development for kids and teens.

Frequently Asked Questions

Now that you've had a first look at what I'm proposing in this book, you may have some natural doubts: it may seem a little daunting. Let's look at some questions and even objections that parents have expressed to me, and I'll respond to them.

If my children are having difficulties, does that mean I'm not a good person?

No, it doesn't. Parents who want help with their children are people of good character. The problem is that we don't always show our best side to our kids. As I mentioned earlier, we may unconsciously channel poor behaviours that our own parents used, and beyond that, as working parents we are often too busy or too tired to summon our best. And it's partly about *awareness*: parents aren't always conscious of how they come across to their kids, and how with a few small tweaks, they can learn to model the characteristics they would like to see in them. That's what modelling with intention is all about. Lastly, our children's problems aren't all about us. We live in a culture and a time that influences children in all sorts of ways, and we don't always know how to counteract the negative ones. The good news is that you *do* have what it takes, and with a little direction and a clear plan, you *can* harness your own character and use it as a powerful force for the good of your children. Once you start to see the positive changes that will happen in your kids, you will be encouraged and energized to keep modelling intentionally.

I'm afraid I'll feel phony if I suddenly start parading "good" behaviour and talking about these ten virtues. Almost like I'm putting them on, just for show.

You're right to say that good character needs to be authentic; it shouldn't just be something we "put on" to manipulate our children. The thing is, the character attributes that we're talking about are *self-affirming.* Once you start to consciously model them and see how that makes you feel and how it makes your children feel (and act), you will quickly realize that you are getting in touch with something very deep that is really you. Rather than a trip into alien territory, it will feel more like coming home.

Do I have to know it all before I start? What if I can't do a perfect job of modelling character?

You don't have to be perfect or know it all. You have many talents as a parent and you love your children. You can and will learn this new skill as you go, and your own family will help you find your way. Remember, this isn't a competition! You aren't being compared to any other parent; what matters is that you'll soon find you are learning and making progress, and the improvements you see will validate your effort and spur you on. You will discover that your daily life with your children is full of opportunities that you didn't see before; there's a lot of "low-hanging fruit" to pluck! All you need to bring is a desire for change and a vested interest in your children's future. I'll supply my experience, my passion, and the framework for you to follow.

What if my kids are already teenagers? Is it too late?

It may be more difficult but it's *never* too late, and it's better to try to improve things at whatever point than to give up on yourself and your children. If you develop a new way of communicating with your children when they are teenagers, they may be a little thrown off by the foreign language and new approach, but a jolt may be just what they need to bring about positive change.

I don't have time to devote to this plan. Is it worth it?

As I'll discuss later in the book: better to devote some time to this new approach now than to spend the greater time that may be required later on to turn wayward kids around. By taking the time to learn new skills, you are investing in your children's future. It's easy to have money withdrawn from your bank account each month for RESP contributions. It's harder to take the time to read a book like this, to meet with your partner and your family, but it's more worthwhile than all the financial gain in the world. You and your children will be richer in more important ways.

The initial time commitment to this program is significant—as you learn the tools and follow the steps laid out. Once you're on your way, the time commitment becomes less. In any case, you will find that you actually *enjoy* the ride. You will realize that the time devoted to your family is more worthwhile than anything else in your life—work, friends, and the rest.

My spouse (or kid) is not on board.

Sometimes it takes some convincing to get everyone on board and certain people may never be quite as committed to the plan as others. Even if they sit on the periphery, that is okay. To make an analogy: some people come to counselling sessions not really wanting to be there. It usually takes less than an hour, so long as the therapist is empathic, encouraging, supportive, and acknowledging, to convince them that they would like to return. Who doesn't like to be part of a supportive environment?

I feel that I am a good person and that I try my best, but my kids don't seem to notice. Or: my kids are just like their

father (or mother); no matter how hard I try, they follow his (or her) lead more than mine.

Try not to be discouraged by your children not seeming to notice or care about the effort and care you put into parenting. Also, try not to be discouraged by your child seeming to follow your partner's "bad" example. Even if it's hard to believe, I can assure you (based on all the confidential conversations I have had with children who "don't care") that they really do care and that they really do notice what is going on. Children are so wise to their parents' strengths and weaknesses. Even when they get angry at you for being so "good" and for always expecting them to do the "right" thing, they secretly think that you're really great and doing an outstanding job, and they appreciate your heart and soul, even though they may not always show it. With regard to feeling that your partner is sabotaging your best intentions or that he or she may be influencing your children in the wrong direction, this is where communication needs to come in. Engaging in the activities and strategies I suggest in this book is a great way of better understanding one another. Sometimes a partner who is sabotaging another's intentions may actually be feeling discouraged. They may actually be feeling as if they can't live up to the "good" partner's ideals and therefore, like a child, may try to get attention by acting out as the "bad" child. I talk in Chapter 5 about how to partner with your co-parent, even when it isn't easy.

Your program sounds too boiler-plate: how can it apply to my unique family?

At every stage, I encourage you to illuminate the material with your own best lights—to decide, for example, which of the ten character attributes can do the most good in your family, and to add other attributes that you feel are valuable. Since every family is different, the sentences in my script are not complete.

The blanks are there so that you can fill in your own words. In Chapter 9, The Family Plan, I offer you key lines and the framework. You can then build and improvise within the script that I have started.

The processes of modelling and partnering will always have a unique outcome, because no two parents and no two children are the same. Don't worry; you'll always be a pioneer in the terrain of your own family!

Ultimately, you will learn and grow as a parent by reading this book. You will develop more confidence as you work within a framework and a plan. You will feel that you are moving in the right direction and be proud of the commitment you have made and the time you have taken to change your behaviour, so that you are consistently modelling what you want to see in your children.

Along with the positive changes that you'll see at home, you'll have an impact on your children's lives outside of their safety nets. Helping children learn how to behave with character enhances the lives of everyone they come into contact with. As parents continue to model good traits and children learn how behave with character, there will be a reduction in acts of violence and disrespect to people and property. Children will be less likely to bully and more inclined to put themselves into other people's shoes before doing or saying hurtful things. Children will want to do what is right and will see the difference between honesty and dishonesty, responsibility and irresponsibility, respect and disrespect.

Being equipped with a tool box of strategies and ideas, and knowing the direction you are headed, will help you feel better about the power and influence you have for good. Once you have a strong vision of which characteristics are crucial to your family, and a clear plan broken down into manageable pieces about how to model them, you will feel better about yourself as a parent, and more confident about being able to raise good people.

I hope to inspire you to open your eyes to this amazing opportunity to learn and grow as a family. My goal is to help you define where you are now and what direction you need to go, and then to get you en route towards raising your children to be the kind of people you know they can be.

Part One

Chapter 1

Taking a Stand: Defining and Modelling Your Core Values

"Good, honest, hard-headed character is a function of the home. If the proper seed is sown there and properly nourished for a few years, it will not be easy for that plant to be uprooted."
—George A. Dorsey

Before laying the foundation from which our children can grow, we need to define our core beliefs and values in relation to the ten character attributes (or others of your choice) and then decide what it is that we most want to model. In this chapter, I will provide you with the tools to begin this process of self-evaluation. We'll also look at some specific situations that can help hone your sense of your values as a parent, and then I'll provide some pointers to get you started on the modelling path.

Let's begin by reviewing ten attributes, with an example of how a parent can influence by modelling each one.

Responsibility
You get up in the morning to get the kids out of bed, make school lunches, and get them to school even though you didn't get to bed until 2 a.m. (you weren't partying but were working on your finances!).

Respect
You consistently arrive at appointments as scheduled, out of consideration for the other person's time.

Initiative
You call the other parents in your child's class to take up a collection to buy their teacher an end-of-the-year gift.

Integrity
You don't get manipulated into letting your child go to a party (where you suspect there will be little or no supervision) just because "everyone else is going."

Honesty
You tell the cashier that she has given you too much change.

Fairness
You let your children know the consequences of their behaviour in advance rather than arbitrarily assigning a punishment in the heat of the moment.

Courage
You sit in your car as a passenger the first time your teen sits behind the wheel and takes your car on the road.

Perseverance
You sit patiently next to your child and explain the math homework in different ways until he or she understands it.

Empathy

You see a child who has fallen off his bike by the side of the road and you stop to ask if he is alright or needs you to call someone to get him.

Optimism

You help your teen visualize a successful performance when he has cold feet about his part in the school play (and you remind him that preparation will build confidence!).

Where Do You Stand?

If you were lucky enough to have been born into a family where traits such as respect, fairness, and integrity were modelled for you, you may feel pretty comfortable with modelling these traits more intentionally to your own children. If, however, your parents treated each other disrespectfully, if they were unfair when disciplining you, if they often said one thing but did another, then modelling these characteristics may feel more foreign to you. In this case, you may need to persevere, and develop greater patience with yourself as you seek to model the attributes that you value. Never give up hope. The very fact that certain traits were missing from your parents' behaviour may help you set your own priorities.

As a way of defining which of the characteristics are most important to you, I suggest that you rank the list of ten in order of importance—with one being the most important and ten being the least. Before you do, let me clarify. I'm not implying that these virtues have to compete with each other—there is room for all of them. They are all valuable, and they reinforce each other. What I'm suggesting is that you ask yourself, in the context of your own family and your own self, which characteristics you want to put the most time and energy into modelling.

Focus particularly on what may be most needed in your family. For example, a parent may realize that her family members, for the most part, are responsible—they call home when they are going to be late, complete projects they have promised to take care of, and tidy up after themselves. Perhaps, however, the family is not so strong in the area of courage. The parent may realize that each avoids confrontation, and that many of the family members shy away from taking part in situations beyond their comfort zone. Realizing this, the parent may choose to put courage on top of the list of attributes to work on.

Here, in random order, is the list for you to rank:

Honesty
Respect
Responsibility
Integrity
Fairness
Initiative
Empathy
Courage
Perseverance
Optimism

I would encourage you to add any important attributes that you feel are needed to supplement the list. Suggestions I've heard include altruism, humility, generosity, compassion, tolerance, prudence, and flexibility.

Are You on the Same Page?

After ranking the attributes, ask your spouse or partner (if you are co-parenting) to do the same independently. Then compare your rankings to see what differences you bring to the table regarding each of the characteristics.

Again, this isn't a competition. It's more a chance to gain insight into the hopes and desires each of you has for your family. Let's say that you ranked honesty as number one. Along with believing that some or all of your family members need to work on this trait, you will also likely see that experiences growing up in your family of origin affect your ranking. Thinking back, you may realize that dishonesty in your parents' relationship has made you more sensitive to people being honest with one another. Or, if you've ranked optimism as number one, you may reflect on how much it meant to you when your parent saw the future as being bright, even during difficult times. Since your partner's life experiences may be quite different to yours, he or she may have ranked the characteristics differently. When you share your choices with each other and the reasons you made them, you get to know a new dimension of each other and make it possible for the two of you to function better as a team. The goal is not to reject either person's point of view: it is to pool your resources and create a shared definition of the values you want yourselves and your children to have.

Exploring Specific Moral Scenarios

As part of getting to know more about your values as parents, it can be useful to look at more concrete moral situations and imagine what your response would be. I will suggest some examples that you can talk about, and you can also prepare a few questions of your own. They may begin with "What would you do if . . . ?"

For example, one parent may ask the other, "What would you do if our child, at the age of five, picked up a small toy in a store and left with it in her hand?" Let's say that the other parent responds with something like "Well, at her age, she probably wouldn't be stealing intentionally. Since we've already left the store, I would just take her home with it but not make a fuss about her stealing it." The parent asking the question may agree that her child would not have intentionally stolen the toy. She may also agree with not making a big fuss or calling it "stealing." However, she may feel strongly that, in order to model attributes such as honesty, fairness, respect, and responsibility, she would want to handle the situation differently.

She might suggest that following the incident they could talk to their child about not taking toys out of a store without paying for them first, and then return to the store, either to pay for it or give it back. Ultimately, if the couple agrees that honesty, respect, responsibility, and fairness are important attributes to model, they will be able to agree on a way that they could mutually handle the situation so that their child receives the same message from both of them.

Of course we can't anticipate and formulate rote responses for every situation that may arise, but with open discussion and ongoing communication, couples can be better prepared to be on the same page.

Here are some more examples to talk about, keyed to specific character attributes. Please tailor the "facts" so that they reflect your own family as much as possible. Remember that reasonable people can have different takes on these issues. The goal as parents is to respect each other's opinions and to try to reach a consensus or compromise that will work for you as a team.

Perseverance

"What would you say or do if our son, at 16, decided to drop out of school?"
(Or: "What would you do if our son, at 18, decided not to pursue higher education but go in search of a job at a retail outlet?")
Depending on past experience, two parents might respond differently. A mother who was raised in a home where education was of utmost importance and where everyone earned university degrees might have a hard time with her son following a different path. A father whose family members seldom completed high school may be on a totally different wavelength. Neither is wrong, but raising a question like this brings to light their differences/similarities and forces them to consider this real-life issue prior to it happening.

Respect

"What words are you comfortable tolerating at home? Are you okay with our children telling us to shut up? What about swearing? What about swearing outside of the home, with friends?"

I always laugh (inside) when I hear a parent say, "Don't let me ever catch you using that word again!" I can just imagine the child thinking, "I'll make sure you never *catch* me again. Can't promise that I won't use it again, though."

"Are you okay with our children putting their elbows on the table? Talking with their mouths full?"

Wouldn't it be great if couples discussed these questions even before they had children?

Responsibility

"Do you think that we are being responsible parents if we allow our underage teenagers to smoke cigarettes and drink alcohol in our company?"

Some parents prefer that their children drink and smoke in front of them. They say that since they know the kids are likely to experiment, they would prefer to be close by to catch them if they fall. The dilemma they face is how to come across as being responsible as they're watching their children break the law. Issues of fairness, honesty, respect, and integrity can also come in here . . . talk it over and see what you come up with.

"Is gratuitous violence and sex really going over our six-year-old's head or are we doing him an injustice by allowing him to sit with us when we are watching programs with mature themes on television?"

This is a very important question to explore. You may be interested in knowing how one mom handled her daughter's interest in watching a movie that she felt contained subject matter that was too mature. You'll find Georgia's story in Chapter 2 on learning (and teaching) from others' actions.

Fairness

"What do you think we would/should do with our two-year-old who is not able to share?"

This question could trigger a valuable discussion about children's developmental stages, and the need to keep expectations in line with normal behaviour, which at age two doesn't commonly include sharing.

Courage

"What would you do if our ten-year-old refused to sit in the dentist's chair?"

I have heard so many opinions on this. One parent will say that there is no choice, that dental care is not optional, and that if necessary, she will hold her child down. Another parent may relate to (or even share) the fear of being in a dental chair and want to prepare and desensitize the child to the experience in advance, find a paediatric dentist who is best equipped to handle a fearful child, or even suggest having the child put to sleep for the procedure. One parent may consider it weak to show such fear; another may recognize this as normal fear for a ten-year-old (and older!).

These examples are just suggestions. I'm sure you can think of your own situations that strike you as relevant and/or difficult, that you'll want to think about and discuss. They may include issues related to pirating movies and music, pre-marital sex, drugs, and abortion, for example.

When you reach the stage (coming in Part Two) of holding family meetings and guiding your children through examining their own values, it will make things easier if you and your spouse have talked over some of these issues and found common ground, in the form of agreement or compromise. The practice you gain in understanding and respecting each other's values, even when they diverge, will help you show the same respect for your children's points of view, which may, by the way, contain some surprises—sometimes kids are more old-fashioned than their parents!

Even when you and your partner haven't been able to reach agreement on a certain issue, the situation doesn't have to be a disaster. It's okay for your children to see that their parents don't agree on everything; after all, you aren't clones of each other. What *won't* help your kids is for you to be combative or undermining of each other's positions. Part of modelling respect is acknowledging others' beliefs and being open to hearing them, even if they aren't what you think is "right."

Looking at Your Own Behaviour

Now that you've begun to explore the values that are most important to you both, this is a good time to consider whether or not your *own* behaviour reflects them. Do your children *know* which characteristics are most important to you? Have you communicated that to them in a positive way? Do a little survey of your children's behaviour. In the areas where they seem to fall short (some of which may be the ones you ranked highest in importance), ask yourself whether there are parallels between their behaviour and yours. If there are, that is a clue that better, more conscious modelling will make a big difference.

An interesting angle on this was given to me by Kathleen Redmond,* founder of the Centre for Character Leadership just north of Toronto. Redmond says that when she was growing up, parents were seldom accountable to their children and if children ever disagreed with what their parents said, they were told that they had no right to contradict their elders. Only the children were held accountable for their actions.

Nowadays, Redmond believes that "parents recognize that sometimes what they are doing is not producing the results they want. Parents find it difficult to measure their own behaviour but they can make a great start by observing the behaviour of their children and asking 'Am I happy with this result?' And if not, 'Can I figure out what I need to do differently in order to ensure that I am modelling the right behaviour for these kids?' Holding themselves, as well as their children, accountable to clearly defined standards creates the best conditions for success."[1]

Starting to Model Intentionally

If you've worked through this chapter so far, you are probably feeling a heightened awareness of a whole aspect of your family's life: the aspect of values. You may have a growing sense that a whole lot of what has been going on with your children is suddenly becoming clearer, that there's a way to penetrate the confusion and begin to steer things in the right direction. Your values "antennae" are suddenly vibrating with new intensity, bringing you new data about exactly which behaviours in yourself and your children you want to work on, and which character traits are most relevant. You're seeing all sorts of opportunities to make a change for the better.

It's never too soon to begin utilizing this new awareness, by deliberately modelling to your children the characteristics you

* Kathleen Redmond is a stepmother to two grown women and is an author and executive coach.

have selected. So make a start. When you see a good opportunity to exhibit one of the attributes that you've chosen as important, go ahead and grab it.

And here are some pointers for a successful takeoff:

- At the beginning there's a tendency to tell yourself, "Today will be different. I am going to be the most patient, most responsible, most respectful, and most fair parent in the world." Hold on . . . it's great that you're excited and enthusiastic, but take a deep breath. Take it slow. If you run too fast at the beginning of the race, you'll run out of energy along the way. And if you set your expectations too high, you may be disappointed and give up. What you're beginning is a new way of shaping your own behaviour, so ease into it gradually. This plan requires a lifestyle change.
- Enrich your family interactions with the new vocabulary of character words. Look for opportunities to try them out on your children. You may find that they pick them up rather quickly; children's brains love new words to chew on, and the concepts follow soon after.
- Pause before you respond to situations; give yourself time to process. If you find yourself about to slip into an old pattern of behaviour, remove yourself. You don't have to give your children answers right away. You are entitled to ask for a few minutes (or hours) to think about what they are requesting, or away from what has just happened. Use the time to formulate your response and choose your words more carefully. Take time out to think things through. But always return to resolve the situation, so issues don't get swept under the rug.
- Sometimes you'll replay a scene that just took place and realize that you were channelling something from your own parents' playbook that no longer fits the parenting approach you've

chosen. Or that you simply missed a fine opportunity to model something positive. That's okay. The fact that you are now consciously noticing such things is a huge advance: next time you'll avoid the mistake. You may even want to let your children know that you are not proud of the way you reacted and share that if you had the chance to rewind and do it over, you would have reacted differently.

- Think positively. Often, we think about reacting in kind: "This is a negative situation, so I'll react negatively." When you're about to get angry or discouraged or authoritarian, think to yourself: *which character attribute would turn this situation around?* Good character is all about acting from strength, not from a weak or defensive posture. So look for the strong move, the words or actions that resolve the situation while showing how a person of character deals with life. You'll find that you are empowered. As one mom told me, after modelling more intentionally she realized that she was the pulse of her family: her tempo and behaviour affected how everyone else in the family behaved. It was both exhilarating and overwhelming for her to realize the incredible influence she commanded.
- Don't worry about results in the early days, or try to elicit a reaction from your kids. Results aplenty will come soon, as will reactions! And later on you'll be holding family meetings that will allow all parties to hear fully from each other. Consider whether you want to tell the children about the changes you are going to be making right away, or if you just want to start modelling more consciously and talk about it later.
- Practise good character even when the kids are not around.

I spoke in the Introduction about the worry that a parent may have about a change of behaviour coming off as somehow inauthentic. Let me say a little more about that. You may be concerned that by suddenly pretending to be responsible if you are typically not, taking initiative when you tend to be more of a follower, or persevering even though your tendency is to give up, your children may feel that you are pretending to be someone you are not. If you suddenly switch from seeing the glass half empty to the glass half full, if you suddenly start responding to unsolicited telemarketers with a courteous, "I'm busy right now, please call another day," as opposed to hanging up without saying goodbye, the kids may indeed find it odd.

However, if you gradually begin to behave differently and intentionally model what you want to see in your children, the changes in your behaviour will become second nature as you continue practising them. You will be encouraged to see your children cleaning up after themselves by taking their drink and popcorn containers out of the movie theatre, because you led by example. Even simple gestures such as placing the shopping buggy back in the designated area of the parking lot models putting things back where we found them—something we often stress to our children. In all these cases, pointing out what we are doing ("Let's be sure to put this cart back where it belongs") increases the likelihood that kids will pick up on, and emulate, our behaviour.

Dr. Thomas Lickona,* often called the father of character education, put this point in an excellent way. He said, "Practise is key. That's because a guiding principle is the idea, going back to Aristotle, that virtues are not mere thoughts; they are habits we develop by performing virtuous acts."[2] Every time you consciously apply an attribute of good character, you root it more firmly in your own moral fibre.

* Thomas Lickona is an author, developmental psychologist, and professor of education emeritus at the State University of New York in Cortland, where he directs the Center for the 4th and 5th Rs (Respect and Responsibility).

Short & Sweet

- Before laying the foundation from which our children can grow, we need to define our core beliefs and values in relation to the ten crucial characteristics and then decide what it is that we most want to model in our family.
- Once you and your partner have decided which of the characteristics are most important to each of you, compare your rankings to learn more about each other's values and beliefs.
- Along with your partner, go through some specific moral situations that could arise and discuss how you would handle each.
- With open discussion and communication about values, couples can pool their resources, find common ground, and be better prepared to be on the same page.
- Think about whether or not *your* behaviour is a reflection of the characteristics that are most important to you both. Do your children *know* which characteristics are most important to you? Do you know which are most important to them?
- Think about the way in which your children behave: Is their behaviour a reflection of the characteristics that you value most? Do you see any parallels between their behaviour and yours?
- If you gradually begin to behave differently and model what you want to see in your children, the changes in your behaviour will become second nature as you continue practising them.

Chapter 2

Life's Lessons: Learning by Observing

"When you teach your son, you teach your son's son."
—The Talmud

Demonstrations of character don't always have to feature you. As you work on making yourself a good model for your children, I want to point out another resource that is available, which you can use not only to explore what values you believe in, but also to teach your children what character—good and bad—means. That resource is the rich and varied behaviour of other people.

Part of how we raise our own ethical awareness is by observing others, deciding what feels right and wrong, and then modelling/teaching accordingly. When we look at others' behaviours through the lens of values, we learn about ourselves. We learn what we believe is important and what we do or don't like. Although judging others is not typically condoned, when done in this context it can be part of our learning—and teaching process. In tandem with our increased *self*-awareness, noticing how character is portrayed by others can provide great object lessons to *share* with our children and can help them learn from what they see every day.

For example, as you observe a person holding a door open so that someone laden with groceries can enter, you may think, "That's a nice gesture." If you are with your children, you can use that behaviour as an example of what you hold in high regard by saying what you are thinking out loud. Conversely, if someone acts disrespectfully, you can comment on this too. If your child's friend leaves your home without saying goodbye or thank you, you might mention something like "It's disrespectful not to say goodbye or thank you" to your child. Bite your tongue rather than throw in "I hope that you always use your manners." Even without this addition, your child will have received the message—loud and clear!

As you walk through your day, you'll find that there are many opportunities to point out positive and negative models to your children. When you receive good customer service at a store or when someone returns something you have loaned, you can be appreciative and acknowledge their considerateness—both to the doer and to your children.

If you notice a vandalized billboard along the highway, graffiti on the wall of a building, a homeless man being stepped over, a bus driver staring ahead as a mother navigates her way onto his bus with her child in a stroller, an elderly man being honked at as he cautiously crosses the street, share your observations with your children. Engage them in discussions to get them thinking about what you've all seen. As adults, we have a million thoughts running through our heads every day. Many we don't express out loud. There are so many opportunities for your children to learn from what you see and think.

Even though we may want to protect our children from the big bad world, there will be times when we're in their company and hear stories of random acts of violence towards innocent people, of police raids that uncover millions of dollars of illegal drugs, or of people being shot and thrown from moving cars on the highway. Or we may be standing with our children in an elevator and have no place to hide when fellow passengers use expletives we'd rather our children not be exposed to. Instead of pretending that it hasn't happened, we can again use these experiences as springboards for age-appropriate discussions with our children.

As they grow in age and maturity, we need to trust that they will make good decisions based on our coaching. Ultimately, we need to let them stand alone. If we have done a good job, they will have developed a solid social and moral conscience by the time they are ready for greater independence. Then we can step back knowing that they will make sound choices.

Many parents prohibit their children from watching certain television programs or movies for fear of what they might learn from watching others. I am not advocating that you expose your children to gratuitous violence or inappropriate content just to have something to talk about. But perhaps exposure to some of what is popular with their peer group, even if you have concerns about some of its content, may allow for teachable moments.

For example, one mother (Georgia) told me about the time her daughter Madison, at age six, asked to show a particular movie, popular with her peers, at her upcoming birthday party. Georgia was usually hesitant to expose her daughter to subject matter which she thought was too mature. However, after chatting with me, she began thinking about how she might unintentionally be keeping her child too cocooned: Madison's bubble would burst some day and she might be lost in a world she had had very little exposure to. So she suggested that they watch the movie together.

When they sat down to watch it, Madison was bursting with excitement. She knew all the words to the songs in the movie (one of the carpool moms played them on the way home every day) and Madison wanted to see what the singers looked like. Georgia had watched the movie while Madison was at school so that she could prepare for their time together. She knew that much of the content would go over her daughter's head but that was even more concerning: she worried that Madison would absorb or maybe even imitate without fully understanding it. Madison asked a lot of "why" questions and her mom stopped the movie several times to explain a character's words or behaviour. Even though Madison didn't get the underhanded, manipulative behaviour of one character trying to purposely sabotage another's opportunity to be in the spotlight, Georgia stopped the video to talk to her about what was happening. In language her daughter could understand, Georgia explained that one girl who was always picked to play the leading role in the school plays was upset and jealous that another girl was trying out. Actually, Georgia was impressed at Madison's ability to translate the character's experiences into something she could relate to in everyday life. "You mean like when my friend was upset when the teacher asked me to take the attendance to the office even though it was usually her job?" she asked.

Georgia asked age-appropriate questions to help Madison understand the relevance of what she was watching. In response to one character rigging the situation so that she would win, mom asked daughter, "Was it fair to organize two events on the same day so that she couldn't enter the competition?" to which daughter replied, "No, that's like cheating on a game."

The models in popular movies can be tough acts to go against. Not to say that life has to be so serious or that you can't just enjoy a movie, but especially with young children, it is good to be cognizant of the subtle messages they are picking up on and how what appears to be going over their heads might well be absorbed and regurgitated when you least expect it. Look for opportunities to discuss how movie or TV characters communicate with one another and treat one another, and what messages are being shared.

Once children develop strong character, they are more likely to reject poor behaviour when they are exposed to it. They have their own point of view, it's really *theirs*, and it's a delight when they express it to you. So a teen may share frustrations and concerns about peers cheating during tests, using alcohol and drugs, and behaving disrespectfully towards their teachers. That demonstrates strong values coming from within, not least of them the courage and integrity to stick to one's personal beliefs and values, at the risk of not fitting in. When your child shares such feelings with you, take the opportunity to say things like "That showed a lot of integrity. You stood your ground and didn't cheat, even though some of your peers did."

You've started modelling character in your own behaviour—leading by example. You've also begun to derive object lessons from others' behaviour, even when it's not so admirable. So you're off to a good start. Though your momentum will build steadily, there may still be moments when old parenting habits try to tempt you off your new path. In particular, it's sometimes hard to remember the future when faced with the demands of this moment. I'll talk about how to surmount that in the next chapter.

Short & Sweet

- Part of how we continue to learn about values is by observing others, deciding what feels right and wrong, and teaching our kids accordingly.
- Instead of pretending that "bad" behaviour doesn't exist, use your observations and experiences as springboards for age-appropriate discussions with your children.
- Movies and TV shows that contain questionable messages or are too advanced for your child, if watched together, can offer great chances to talk about values.

Chapter 3

Parenting Today for Tomorrow

"Don't worry that children never listen to you; worry that they are always watching you."
—Robert Fulghum

In this chapter I want to inspire you to think long term. Our children are influenced by everything we do and say, even when we don't have character modelling in mind. And sometimes we try to make kids do what makes today easier, instead of what will make tomorrow better. We may discourage specific behaviours and attributes without realizing how beneficial they might be later on—with the proper direction and modelling—when our children are adults. By the end of this chapter, you may celebrate the knowledge that some of your child's more challenging behaviours may hold him or her in good stead later in life.

Of course we all say and do things that we regret later. A real person isn't perfect and neither is a parent. As parents we don't have to be perfect, we just have to try our best, remembering that allowing our children to observe how we deal with our own character failures is incredibly valuable.

Encouraging Future Virtues

I remember one evening when my colleague Lana Feinstein and I were leading our parenting group, she brought an article that she had written. It was entitled *Parenting Today for Tomorrow.* In it, she wrote that the work of parents extends far beyond their world today, into their child's world of tomorrow. After reading it out loud, she asked the parents, "Which characteristics do you want your children to possess as adults and what are you doing today to help your children become the people you hope they will be tomorrow?"

This sparked an exciting discussion during which the parents exchanged their thoughts and ideas. One mom realized that although she wanted her child to grow to be a person with integrity and to stand up for what he believed in, she had nevertheless recently discounted his desire to become a vegetarian. Another wanted her daughter to grow up to become a respectful person, but admitted that when she called her "a liar" and "lazy" she wasn't modelling respect herself. One of the fathers remarked that by not including his children in decisions, he was teaching them to be passive followers, not leaders. He recognized that by becoming more democratic and open to compromise and negotiation, he would be allowing his children to practise being diplomatic, assertive, and persistent, all characteristics he wanted his children to possess as adults.

Another evening, Lana and I presented the group with a worksheet that we titled "Long-term Parenting." We divided the sheet down the middle and created two columns. On the left-hand side of the page, under column A, we listed several characteristics such as bossy, demanding, obedient, nosy, and wanting to please. On the other side of the page, under column B, we listed other characteristics such as persistent, self-confident, curious, compliant, and dependent. We asked the parents to circle the characteristics in column A that they would be glad to see in their children. Of those listed above, the majority of parents circled obedient and wanting to please. On the other side of the page, we asked the parents to circle the characteristics under column B that they hoped their children would possess as adults. Of those characteristics, the majority of parents circled persistent, curious, and self-confident, all of which were, ironically, the opposite of the qualities they were glad to see in their children. An adult who shows persistence may have been called a "demanding" child. An adult who shows curiosity may have been a "nosy" child. An adult who is self-confident may have been labelled a "bossy" child.

This was an eye-opening exercise for many of the parents, who hadn't realized that some "negative" behaviours or attributes in children may be perceived as "positive" in adults, and that some "positive" behaviours or attributes in children may be perceived as "negative" in adults.

After completing the exercise, the parents were unanimous in their conclusions. Everyone agreed that they wanted to raise their children to be, among other things, self-confident and independent. They also agreed that they wanted their children to be courageous, take initiative, and show compassion towards others. They realized that they needed to proceed with caution when trying to extinguish certain of their children's challenging behaviours.

Along with considering that more challenging childhood behaviours may, with the proper direction, lead to positive characteristics when our children grow to be adults, it is also important to consider how our coping strategies as parents can sometimes undermine the characteristics we want to instil in our children.

Authority vs. Respect

How to discipline has long been an important issue for parents. Depending on whom you talk to or which books you read, you will note great differences in opinion. From gentle reminders to time-outs to spanking, parents want to know what works. When I offer my opinion to clients, I first ask myself, "Is this solution a short-term Band-aid or will it be a long-term strategy to help raise a responsible, caring, and respectful human being?"

For example, from a certain perspective, spanking works. It immediately stops a child from behaving a certain way. So, for some, this may be considered a successful way to deal with a more challenging child. My belief, however, is that spanking is short-term gain for long-term pain. The short-term gain is that the behaviour stops. The long-term pain is that, among other things, spanking leads to children feeling angry and resentful. It falls under the authoritarian style of parenting, which often creates an environment within which children feel as if they are being treated unjustly, unfairly, and disrespectfully. Spanking also teaches a child that someone who is more powerful, bigger, and stronger should be allowed to strike someone who has less power and strength. Instead, a parent who comes up with a logical consequence that is directly related to the problem at hand models fairness and respect.

Let's take a quick example. A parent yells downstairs for a child to "get off the computer." After several "How many times do I have to ask you to get off the computer?" the parent charges towards the child, pulls him out of his chair, and hits him on the behind. Then says, "Now, go to your room. I'm sick and tired of having to ask you a million times to get off."

An alternative: the same parent sits with the child at a quiet time. "I've noticed that you have a hard time getting off the computer when I ask you to," the parent says. "How do you think that we can resolve this?" They discuss some of the reasons for limiting computer time, such as the value of other activities that might get short-changed. They decide to set a timer at the side of the computer and when it goes off, the child agrees to turn off the computer. They also determine that a logical consequence to his not getting off the computer is that he will lose his computer privileges the following day. The logic of this is that if the child cannot show responsibility by sticking to the agreed-upon plan, then he cannot enjoy the privilege of going on the computer the following day. He can try again the day after.

Not only does the latter approach model respect and fairness on the parent's part, but it gives the child the opportunity to handle responsibility: the responsibility of making a choice, and experiencing consequences. It allows children to figure out for themselves how they would like to behave, and why. "What do I want to do here? If I don't heed the timer, I'll lose computer access for a whole day." Thus the "logical consequence" approach leads to the child *choosing* the right behaviour, not having it forced upon him or her. (A word of caution: make sure that you too are modelling appropriate use of the computer.)

A similar point applies to modelling in general. Leading by example has more lasting results than ordering kids around. An authoritarian approach may make kids do (or stop doing) something at that moment, but it has a severe drawback. It doesn't bring about *voluntary* good behaviour. It may make the parent feel like he or she is in control, but the truth is a little different. If you expect your child to obey you *just because you are a parent*, you'll get involuntary (and temporary) obedience at best. Your children may "respect" your orders because you have more power, but you haven't earned their real respect in the sense of the character trait. You aren't really in control, because rebellion or sabotage can arise at any time—especially when you're not around. By contrast, when your children change their behaviour because they have seen the good example you set in your own behaviour, they are proceeding *freely*, from their own sense of what is worthy. Now that is real change that will last.

How One Dad Turned Himself Around

This chapter has been about becoming aware of poor parenting habits, and altering them for good. I want now to showcase the amazing motivating force of one parent's simple realization that if he persisted with his bad behaviour, his children would very likely be "infected" by it in a way that would permanently mar them. The story I'm about to tell shows that even in a fairly grim situation, a real desire to change the future can turn things around.

When Sam called to schedule an appointment to see me professionally, he painted a very bleak picture of his life. He said that he and his wife were separated after many years of conflict and chaos, and that he had custody of their four children, ranging in age from seven to 17. He said that he knew that he was partly to blame for the way his children were behaving, but didn't know how to undo what had already been done. He desperately wanted someone to help him figure out what to do next, and how to connect with his kids. What complicated their situation was that each of the kids had been placed in separate foster care homes over the years and had only recently been allowed to trickle back home. Sam knew that if he didn't change his behaviour as a parent by yelling less and being more consistent and responsible (which included not drinking or using drugs), his younger children might be removed from his care again.

Over the course of a month, I met with his ex-wife, Brenda, and with the children, alone and as a group. Each of the children manifested parts of the turmoil to which they had been exposed and reflected their parents' relationship over the years. The youngest daughter, aged nine, was very aggressive. She threw objects at people and the wall when she was angry, and her teachers reported that she had a difficult time resolving conflict with her peers. Dad admitted that he had, at times, thrown objects when angry. He shared that until they separated, he and his wife fought often and she sometimes hit him.

Sam's 11-year-old son was withdrawn. He found it hard to share his feelings and was bullied by his older brother, who called him a "mouse." Sam admitted that he, at times, had called his son the same. He hadn't thought of this as name-calling until I pointed it out.

Sam's 13-year-old daughter dressed and acted as if she was much older. She made loud, slurping noises as she sucked diet pop through a straw in between her responses to my questions, and her makeup looked as if it had been applied over what remained from the day before. Her red nail polish was chipped and she wore large hoop earrings and high-heeled sandals. She looked like a mini version of her mother. When Brenda, her mother, and I first met, she admitted to dressing provocatively and said she liked to attract attention from men. She shared that this had created a great deal of conflict in their marriage and that she ultimately left to be with someone she met at a dance club.

When I met with Sam's 17-year-old son on his own and asked about rules in the house, he said that there weren't any. He came and went as he pleased and there were no routines or rituals to be followed. When people were hungry, they helped themselves to whatever was in the fridge, and most of the time everyone just "did their own thing." He used alcohol and drugs, and on occasion shared joints with his 13-year-old sister. He said that he knew that mom and dad had used drugs too, and when they were all living together, he could sometimes smell marijuana coming from their bedroom.

After meeting the children, I talked to Sam and his wife separately. I shared my concerns, heard more of theirs, and offered suggestions to create more cohesion. I also talked about modelling with intention and asked each of them to think about what they had modelled in the past, as well as what they hoped to model in the future. I think that Sam had hoped that I could wave a magic wand. But he had the courage to face the truth.

He came to realize that real change would happen for his kids only if it happened in him first. It was a difficult process for him: coming to terms with what he had done and how his children had been affected made him weep.

Now that his children were living with him, Sam realized that he had the greater influence, and developed a plan. Over the course of several months, he created opportunities for connection as a family and modelled better behaviours that trickled from his 17-year-old down. He joined an anger management group to learn more about what triggered his anger and how to deal with it differently. He paired his 13-year-old with a "big sister" who spent time with her and modelled appropriate behaviour and dress. And he vowed to never use drugs again.

The changes Sam made were not easy. But knowing how high the stakes were, he prevailed. He replaced a bad example with a good one, modelling a number of attributes intentionally:

- He modelled responsibility by making his children his priority, and staying clean. Giving up drugs is a lot easier said than done; it will test every character attribute on the list, and probably more. Sam did it. It was hard, and some weeks he attended his support group meetings every day.
- He modelled honesty by not lying to his kids about his former drug use.
- He modelled courage and empathy by being willing to put himself in their shoes, and realizing how difficult it had been for them to live with him and their mother for so many years.
- He modelled integrity and perseverance by saying that he was going to change and then sticking to his word.
- He took initiative by joining a support group.
- He showed more respect towards his children by not yelling and calling them names, and by honouring their need to

have him present—both physically and emotionally. (He also respected their need not to have their mother in their home when she was using.)

Trust takes time to rebuild. But as his children saw him remaining true to his word, they began to believe that he was going to keep on being a more responsible, honest, caring parent. His eldest joined him at the support group to kick his own addiction. And the children began treating each other more respectfully as their father continued to model respect towards them. As Sam noticed changes for the better and became more self-aware, he grew more confident and excited about his plan.

Sam's story is a powerful example of how parents' behaviour and lifestyle affects their children, and how their concern for their kids' future can surmount even huge challenges.

Short & Sweet

- Which characteristics do you want your children to possess as adults and what are you doing today to help your children become the people you hope they will be tomorrow?
- Some negative behaviours or attributes in children may be perceived as positive in adults, and some positive behaviours or attributes in children may be perceived as negative in adults. For example, an adult who shows persistence may have been called a demanding child. So, be careful about wanting to extinguish certain attributes: think long term!
- It is important to consider how our own behaviour and parenting strategies model the characteristics we want to instil in our children.
- Authoritarian parenting may work in the short term, but modelling and using "logical consequences" can lead to real change in your children's behaviour.

- Even in fairly grim circumstances, a parent with courage and desire can change the outcome for his kids, by changing the example he or she sets.

Chapter 4

Modelling as They Grow: From Tots to Teens

"It's not only our children who grow. Parents do too. As much as we watch to see what our children do with their lives, they are watching us to see what we do with ours. I can't tell my children to reach for the sun. All I can do is reach for it myself."

—Joyce Maynard

Parenting, like gardening, requires patience, perseverance, and timing. Seeds take a good while to develop into flowers, and they have different vulnerabilities and needs through their different growth phases. If you don't make time or have the right tools to tend your garden at each stage, then seeds may fail to germinate and flowers could wilt in the hot sun. In the same way, children need your patience and understanding as they grow from infants to toddlers to teens and beyond.

When your child is a newborn, you have no choice but to model responsibility. Newborns cannot fend for themselves and without you they will not survive. Within the first few weeks and months, your infant not only relies on you in order to live, but also develops a sense of the world around him by your response to his needs. The mother who persists with breast-feeding, despite cracked nipples and her baby's difficulty with latching on, is modelling perseverance. The father who, one week after his baby's arrival, returns to work—despite wanting to stay at home with his wife and newborn—is modelling responsibility. Neither parent may intentionally be modelling at the time. In fact, modelling may be the farthest thing from the minds of sleep-deprived parents of a newborn, but they are modelling nonetheless—both as a test of their own character and as role models for their child and his siblings.

As infants grow into toddlers, parents continue to model empathy, responsibility, and perseverance. You may also model optimism, patience, respect, and courage when your toddler is not developing at quite the speed of her peers:

- optimism that he will catch up eventually
- patience if she doesn't catch on as quickly
- respect that everyone develops at his own rate
- courage if she needs special attention while developing.

As children begin to show some independence and assert themselves, parents move into defining limits. As we began to see in the last chapter, learning how to discipline respectfully is a critically important part of modelling respect towards our children. If your three-year-old reaches out to pull the dog's tail and you smack her hand, you likely are not modelling what you would like to see in her. Your approach to discipline should be planned and intentional, just like your approach to modelling.

It's important to make sure that your style is consistent with your values and beliefs. If you believe that fairness, for example, is an important characteristic to model, then arbitrary punishment or rewarding of your children is not consistent with your belief system. Allowing a natural consequence to occur or implementing a logical consequence for certain behaviour would be more in keeping with modelling fairness.

It isn't fair (or effective discipline) to employ rewards and punishments that are unrelated to what the child did. For example, a child who is taken to the toy store after a good report card may like the reward, but there is no connection between the behaviour (working hard and getting good results) and the material reward. More clearly, a child who is punished for getting a bad report card by not being allowed to go to a friend's birthday party that weekend is right when he says, "But that's not fair!" It *isn't* fair for a parent to arbitrarily assign a punitive action that is totally unrelated to the problem, and about which the child had no previous warning.

If the parent was operating in a "fair" mode, he or she would either allow a natural consequence to occur, or implement a logical consequence. A natural consequence would be that a poor report card may cause not moving up to the next grade (but this consequence is seldom heard of these days). How about a logical consequence? Let's suppose the parent has been diligently aware of the child's academic progress all term, has had him or her assessed to make sure that there is no disability impeding his or her ability to do well, and therefore has good reason to conclude that the poor grades have more to do with not spending enough time on schoolwork. A fitting logical consequence (in this case, for a child who spends a lot of time playing electronic games) would be for the parent to advise the child in advance, "I know that you are capable. I also know that you feel you can spend any amount of time on electronic games and still get good grades. Let's establish a consequence if you can't get those grades up." They may decide that a poor report grade would mean that the child's use of games would be monitored and limited for the remainder of the school year.

The years up to age six are the formative years of a child's life. During this time children develop a sense of how stable or rocky their foundation is. Even though they may not process what they are seeing and hearing in the same way as would an older child, they experience everything that is modelled before them and, like sponges, absorb and retain this information for future reference.

That is why, when parents come to talk to me about their child's behaviour, I often ask that they first come without their child. Even though they may not think that their three-year-old is able to comprehend what they are saying, he or she may well be bright and intuitive enough to understand more than a parent might expect. It's never too early to be conscious of what we are doing and saying when our kids are around.

Writer John Hoffman has an interesting take on this. He believes that kids, especially when they are little, act as a *second conscience* for parents. He says, "We know how impressionable they are, so we are perhaps more conscious of being on our 'best behaviour' more of the time. We may think more carefully about the language we use, being courteous, not bad-mouthing people under our breath, and taking the time to stop and look both ways when we cross the street."*

From approximately aged six and up, children become more consciously tuned in to what we are doing and saying. They are quick to point out where we are going wrong or being hypocritical. Being a parent can be a humbling experience. I have learned that I am certainly not always right. When one of my daughters says, "It's not fair," she's often correct. So, instead of saying, "I don't care if it's fair or not. Just do it" (which would not model respect, fairness, or empathy), I say "What do you think would make it more fair?"

* From an interview with John Hoffman, a married father of three grown children, freelance writer, researcher, and blogger.

It's not always easy to stop and listen to what our children are sharing—both because we're so busy and because we may not find what they have to say convenient. But the principle of respect calls on us to do just that, and to make appropriate adjustments based on what we hear.

During the important school-aged years, we can model characteristics that will encourage our children to develop good work habits. We can persevere through difficult tasks—both at home and outside—and take responsibility when things don't go well. We can model responsibility by properly maintaining our homes and making sure that our children are sheltered and don't go hungry. We can model fairness by not taking sides with one child over another, and courage when our children see us face challenges that make us fearful.

Years ago we celebrated our younger daughter's ninth birthday party by having her friends join us at a movie theatre. Unfortunately, when we booked the venue, the organizers had very little availability and so we chose a Friday evening during her birthday month. When she heard that two of her friends could not join us because of Friday evening religious observances with their families, she was bitterly disappointed. I modelled empathy by acknowledging her disappointment, but then saw this as an opportunity to instil the importance of family by saying, "It must have been hard on the parents to not allow their children to attend the birthday party of a good friend. Friday evening dinners are a commitment that they have made to one another and the parents are showing integrity and responsibility by making sure that they continue to spend that time together." I realized that had the parents given in, their children might have seen the exception as a new rule.

As our children grow into teens, there may be a period of rebellion as they assert themselves in the same way that they did as toddlers. The difference, however, is that as a teen, they have more power—both physically and mentally. The teen years can sometimes make us feel as if all of the previous years spent raising our children have been thrown out the window. We blame hormones and friends, the internet, alcohol, and drugs for the changes. While some of these things can of course influence our children, this period of rebellion will likely be short-lived so long as their inner core remains intact and you continue to model what you want to see. Don't give up hope. Remain optimistic and continue to persevere as the parent of a teen.

When Isabel first came to me, she was recently separated from her second husband. Her older children from her first marriage had sailed through their teenage years and were away at university. Her third child, a daughter of 11, was sweet and shy. Danielle sat close to her mother, often with her head on Isabel's shoulder. The recent separation had made Isabel and Danielle even closer than before. Both seemed to be handling the transition well. After a few sessions of discussing changes to their living arrangement and how Danielle felt about spending time alone with her dad, we terminated counselling and agreed to meet only as necessary.

I didn't hear from Isabel until a few years later. Danielle was 14 at the time and Isabel sounded frantic. She said that Danielle was refusing to spend time at her dad's house, that Isabel was being accused of turning Danielle against her father, and that Danielle was hanging out with peers she didn't think highly of. This time, Isabel dragged an unwilling Danielle to see me. Still reticent to open up, Danielle no longer looked as sweet. She sat on a separate couch from her mom. One eye covered by a shock of blue hair, she peered at me from the other. She sneered as her mother talked about the friends she was hanging with and made comments like "What do *you* know, Mother? You're such a goody two-shoes" and "So what if I had a cooler. We were at Carly's house and her parents were upstairs." She denied her mother's concerns that she was smoking marijuana and responded with "Everyone does" when her mother talked about her skipping class at school.

An unwilling participant, Danielle didn't return to my office after that. Isabel, however, became a regular. Every couple of weeks for a year, her visits allowed her to vent and cry. She said that they grounded her, kept her from going insane, and reminded her that it was not her fault that Danielle was being so difficult. My words of encouragement and advice, she said, also helped to give her the strength, courage, and perseverance to continue parenting with integrity.

Danielle is now 17 and in her final year of high school. When I saw her last, she was hanging out in my waiting room. Isabel had come in to see me after a full year's absence and they were going out shopping together after the session. Danielle and I didn't talk much but I could tell that she had softened. Isabel had come in to share how well they were doing. She said that Danielle had come to realize that she and Isabel were on the same team, and that when Isabel asked her not to do something, it wasn't because she wanted power over her, but because she cared about her. Isabel also noted a huge improvement in Danielle's motivation at school: she didn't need to coax her out of bed in the morning any more, and teacher reports were glowing. Once a prickly cactus, Danielle was now allowing her softness to come through again, exposing parts of herself that Isabel had missed. Isabel said that she felt as if they had weathered a rough storm and was happy they had come out intact on the other end. She thanked me for helping her hang on tight, for not giving up hope, and for remaining optimistic that she and her daughter would see this through.

Before we turn to Part Two and the series of family meetings which constitute The Family Plan at the heart of this book, the next three chapters will talk about how you as a parent can team up with partners on three fronts: your co-parent (even if you are not living together), your children, and your children's teachers—all in order to more effectively influence your kids for good.

Short & Sweet

- When your child is a newborn, you have no choice but to model responsibility.
- As infants grow into toddlers, parents continue to model empathy, responsibility, and perseverance.
- Birth to age six are the formative years of a child's life. During this time they develop a sense of how stable or rocky their foundation is.
- During the important school-aged years, we can model characteristics that will encourage our children to develop good work habits and continue to learn more about developing character.
- As our children grow into teens, there may be a period of rebellion as they assert themselves in the same way that they did as toddlers. It's important to hang in there and keep modelling with consistency; your child will come through.

Chapter 5

Handling Conflict with Your Co-Parent (Even after Divorce)

"The greatest gift a father can give his children is to love and respect their mother."
—Author unknown

All couples argue. After all, how many people can live together for years and always agree on everything? When children are added to the mix, couples will likely censor some of the style and content of their disputes. One reason for this: they know that children learn from the way in which they argue and resolve conflict.

This point is documented in an article by Marvin Berkowitz and John Grych.* They write, "As parents can model respect and compassion towards others, so may they model behaviour that is harmful or abusive. For example, parents who resolve disagreements by belittling, coercing, or physically dominating their spouse may teach children that aggression is an appropriate response when their interests conflict with another's. Although children may not imitate the specific behaviours they observe,

* Professor of Psychology at Marquette University, Milwaukee, Wisconsin.

their beliefs and attitudes about how to treat other people may well be shaped by such family experiences. The fact that these 'lessons' are unintended makes them no less powerful."[1]

Lickona also writes about the way we treat each other as spouses, saying this is "something that our children have thousands of opportunities to observe. Our marital behaviours, we can be sure, will imprint themselves on their moral memories." He offers these questions:

- "When we fight, do we fight fair?
- Do we use disrespectful and denigrating language or do we maintain in our words and tone a basic respect, even in the heat of an argument?
- Do we forgive and reconcile soon after, or do we hold on to our anger and resentment?"[2]

How much success parents have in intentionally modelling character, therefore, depends to some extent on how well they get along as a couple. So we owe it to our children to continually examine our relationships with their other parent—whether living in the same house or apart.

Jennifer, one of the parents who participated in the test run of this book's Family Plan, shared concerns about what she and her husband were modelling to their ten-year-old son. She said that she was in her late teens when she met her husband. At the time she thought, "He would make such a great dad." He had lots of experience as a babysitter and she was impressed that he knew how to soothe a crying child.

After dating for six years, Jennifer and Alan married. By the time they had their first child ten years later Jennifer felt that they were basically on the same page with regard to their values and beliefs. Despite this, she didn't always feel that Alan was respectful of their son Anthony's judgments and so she would jump in to defend him. In turn, Alan would feel unsupported by Jennifer and would get defensive. This pattern also applied with their younger child.

In response to these problems, Jennifer made an effort to stop herself from correcting her husband in front of their children. She tried to accept that unless Alan was doing or saying something that was potentially damaging to their children's self-esteem, for example, she needed to avoid interceding. She now says "Alan is who he is" and understands that what he brings out in the children is sometimes going to be different from what she is aiming at.

Since she has tried to step back and analyze her behaviour and then approach Alan only when they are alone, Jennifer has noticed a decrease in fighting in their home and feels that it has become a more respectful environment.

Shari, another parent who participated in The Family Plan, agrees with Jennifer that each parent may model differently and that ultimately "the kids are going to decide what they are going to take from everyone they see." However, she does try to respectfully make her feelings known to her children if their father has done something that goes against what she is trying to encourage. For example, when Tony packed a stray hair dryer that he found in a hotel room and took it home instead of to the Lost and Found, she spoke up. "I don't feel good about Dad taking that," she told the kids. "And I wouldn't have done that myself." Shari says that children will see that there are different sides of the coin—that there are choices to make.

Not all couples are as aware of how much their relationship acts as a model for their children. When my client Terry shared information about the dynamics in their home, she used the word "hate" to describe what she believes her daughter feels towards her. I challenged her casual laugh. I couldn't imagine that she found it funny—especially when her daughter swears at her. At first Terry appeared guarded in my office. It was as if she was wearing a protective suit of armour. She was careful not to show vulnerability. I asked whether her 14-year-old daughter ever saw her cry. She said yes.

I asked whether her daughter softened her manner or showed empathy towards her as a result. "No, she really hates me," said Mom. "In fact, she seems to relish and take pride in hurting me."

"That must be so painful," I acknowledged. "To believe that your child doesn't care when you're in pain."

"Now you're making me cry," she said, reaching for a tissue. I saw her armour melt away.

Another time, with her husband in the room, we explored their marital relationship and how they resolved conflict. I wasn't surprised to hear that the way in which the couple distanced themselves after a fight was identical to the pattern between mother and daughter. In general it emerged that mother and daughter interacted with one another in a very similar fashion to that of the parents. My initial plan had been to meet first with the daughter so that I could understand the source of her anger, then with mom and daughter to foster a healthier relationship between them. But I realized that unless I helped the parents to work on their relationship and to model respect and caring towards one another, it was unlikely that the mother could establish a different relationship with her daughter.

Parents are really good at beating themselves up without any help from me. So, instead of making Terry and her husband feel more guilty about how badly they were affecting their children, I commended them for coming to see me and then helped them explore different ways of relating to one another.

I know that it takes a tremendous amount of courage to be able to face up to the possibility that we—intentionally, or not—are contributing to our children's misbehaviour. It's so much easier to excuse it as a "phase" or say that our child's attitude or belligerence is related to his hanging out with a bad group of kids. However, when we accept the tremendous influence that our relationship as a couple has on our children's behaviour, we give ourselves the key to making positive changes to that behaviour.

Partnering after Divorce

Divorce rocks our children's world and fractures the very foundation that we have laid. According to a 2009 CBC-TV documentary, half of all couple unions in Canada end in divorce—many within 14 years. Some 50,000 more Canadian children are affected each year—and these statistics don't include children from common law relationships. It's not the actual day of separation or the day the divorce papers are signed that concerns me most. After more than two decades of counselling families that have been affected by divorce, my greatest concern is how the children are affected by the *fallout* and *aftermath* of their parents' decision. The amount of harm that results depends on the way in which the parents manage their relationship while living apart, the way in which they model appropriate behaviour towards one another and their children.

I try to help divorced parents model appropriate behaviour towards one another. Although the ideal is for parents to model the same good character as a team, this is often difficult. If you are separated or divorced, work at putting emotion aside and take a hard look at what your words and actions towards one another are teaching your child.

Research confirms the power of post-divorce acrimony. Dr. Marvin Berkowitz says, "We know from the divorce literature that one of the greatest impacts on the kids is how the parents get along with each other after they part. If parents engage in mutual undermining and torture, kids are privy to it and it does psychological damage to them."[3]

Brian, one of the dads who took part in The Family Plan, says that when he got married for a second time, he wanted to make sure that this one was for keeps. He says that he and his wife both wrote their goals down on separate sheets of paper and then compared them. He wanted to know about her aspirations and what mattered to her. He believes it's important that partners not have expectations of one another that can't be delivered. And he affirms that problems in a relationship can be avoided by talking about goals and beliefs even before children arrive.

Having raised children in both his first and second marriages, Brian says that it's difficult when your children are being raised in two different homes by parents who are modelling very different values. Especially if your ex is unwilling to work with you in negotiating similar guidelines. He often feels powerless to create any real change in how the children from his first marriage behave. "I try to give guidance," he says. "I voice my displeasure but I know that it will not make much of a difference." When his 15-year-old daughter left her mother's home to move in with him and his wife, Gayle, she didn't last more than a few weeks. "We have rules about bedtime and cell phones," he says. "We emphasize respect first and also honesty and responsibility. In their mother's home, they come and go as they please. We teach our children that common courtesy is to put things back the way you found them. When my daughter came to stay with us, she threw her laundry on the floor because she was used to the housekeeper picking up after her. In our house, we expect kids to make their beds in the morning."

In the midst of emotional turmoil, hurt and hate often get in the way of modelling characteristics such as fairness, respect, responsibility, and empathy. And even when parents do work at remaining respectful towards their ex-spouse, I hear many divorced parents talk about their ex's trying to sabotage or undermine the good they are trying to instil. For example, one parent told me that she does not allow underage drinking in her home but her ex tells their child that he sees no harm in it.

A client who is a single mom of three recently told me about wanting to teach her 15-year-old about taking greater responsibility. She felt good about how she was modelling character by maintaining a good job and taking care of her family, but was disappointed in her son for not making his lunch or getting up in time for school. On the morning that she was last in to see me, she had driven him to school, as usual, but instead of giving him ten dollars to buy his lunch, she told him he was on his own.* She was tired of telling him to find a job to support his spending habits and reminding him to pack a lunch the night before. So she thought this would teach him a lesson.

When she shared what she had done with her ex-husband and asked if he could do the same on the mornings following sleepovers at his house, he refused. He said that he saw nothing wrong with giving their son lunch money and would not do as requested. He was not willing to discuss the matter any further.

In the end, it is the child who suffers most by receiving opposing messages from his or her parents.

Effort, courage, and a little optimism, however, can make for a more cheerful story. When Kate's 15-year-old son was busted for drinking beer and smoking marijuana with some friends in a back alley, the police called her to pick him up from the station. As she drove back home around midnight, they sat in silence. Kate had a million things going through her head, but was afraid to say anything out loud, for fear of regretting it later. Most of all she longed to say, "Why don't you go live with your father for a while. I've had enough of you." But she bit her tongue, knowing that her son's delinquent behaviour

* Later, we talked about how it might have been better if she had set this up as a logical consequence in advance of dropping him off at school with no money and no lunch. Her son likely saw her strategy as punitive rather as a logical consequence of his behaviour.

of late might be related to being angry at his father and not wanting to talk to him at all.

When she called me the next day, desperate for some advice and direction, I suggested that she speak to her ex-husband and that together with their son, they meet me in my office. She said she feared that her ex would not support her, that he would not feel the situation was as serious as she did, that he might not be as concerned as she was about her son getting high or drunk. She also worried about her son's reaction to having his father present. Despite these concerns, I convinced her of how important it was for their son to see them on the same page regarding this behaviour, and suggested that she, her ex, and I talk on the phone prior to meeting with their son in person.

We did, and Kate was surprised to find that her ex supported her feelings. (If she hadn't made the effort to reach him, she might never have found this out.) Together they determined that new guidelines would be put into effect at both their homes and that son and father would get counselling, to move them towards being able to talk again. When the three met in my office, the father did most of the talking and their son listened. Despite Kate's initial apprehension, it appeared that their son was okay with his father's presence. In fact, he seemed quite relieved to see his parents in the same room, agreeing on the consequences for his behaviour. In some crazy way, he had brought them all closer together. Over time, both parents focused on helping him through their difficult divorce, and agreed on ways to develop his sense of responsibility. As he saw them working together more amicably as co-parents, his behaviour improved too.

Whether living together or apart, it is vital for parents to always think about whether or not they are acting in the best interests of their children, whether their messages are consistent, and whether their behaviour models good character.

Short & Sweet

- Children learn from the way in which you argue and the way you resolve conflict.
- How much success parents have in intentionally modelling character also depends on how well they get along as a couple. So we owe it to our children to continually examine our relationships with their other parent—whether living in the same house or apart.
- When we accept the tremendous influence that our relationship as a couple has on the way that our children behave, we give ourselves the key to making positive changes to that behaviour.
- The amount of harm that results from the aftermath of divorce depends on the way in which the parents manage their relationship while living apart, the way in which they model appropriate behaviour towards one another and their children.
- If you are separated or divorced, work at putting emotion aside and take a hard look at what your words and actions towards your ex are teaching your child.
- Whether living together or apart, it is vital for parents to always think about whether or not they are acting in the best interests of their children, whether their messages are consistent, and whether their behaviour models good character.

Chapter 6

Teaming Up with Your Kids

"The child supplies the power but the parents have to do the steering."

—Benjamin Spock, *Dr. Spock's Baby and Child Care*

Given the chance, our children make great partners in our effort to create a family with character. Especially when exposed to character development at school, they may even be able to teach us something new.

Twelve-year-old Leah, her father, Brian, and her mother, Gayle, recently attended a parent-teacher interview at Leah's school. After taking part in The Family Plan, Brian shared their experience with me. It wasn't a conventional meeting, he said. Instead of the teacher showing them Leah's work, Leah took the lead. During this process, students walk their parents through their folder of work, proudly pointing out progress and answering questions, while their teacher supervises. Brian, familiar with the ten crucial characteristics from the *Character Matters* program, created a mental checklist of how the kids were conducting themselves. He noticed that they were being very responsible and respectful as they conducted the interviews. He also noticed that the students who directed adults to the appropriate room were showing great respect. He noticed that some took initiative and showed empathy when helping a blind lady by taking her hand and leading her.

After the meeting, he reflected on how impressed he was with the results of the character education program at school which he felt had guided the students. He could see that they were in tune with the ten attributes and that they were acting accordingly. "I believe that the kids have the ability to show us the way; to bring us back to what it's all about," he said.

When they returned home, Brian, Gayle, and Leah discussed what he had seen. Brian complimented Leah and her peers on a job well done. Leah felt acknowledged and encouraged to continue behaving in a responsible, respectful manner.

Acknowledging what we see is critically important as we continue to develop character in our children. Also, helping them to become more aware of the process through which they are developing character is invaluable.

For example, after an older sibling has spent time helping his brother or sister with homework, it would be helpful for a parent to ask the older child questions such as "What have you learned about yourself while helping your brother/sister?" The older sibling might then answer with something like "I've learned how to be more patient. I didn't realize how hard it was to pay attention to someone for so long." And in response, the parent might say, "That showed great patience and perseverance on your part." That is the character development part. The best way for a person to grow and understand character is to *experience* it. Once our children have experienced the attribute, then been acknowledged and recognized for modelling it, they are more likely to want to repeat it.

It is vitally important to be honest and genuine when acknowledging your child for showing good character. Children don't always believe us when we say something generic like "You're an honest person." They want specifics. They want to know that you really mean it. For example, they are more likely to trust what you are saying if you recall an incident and describe *how* they acted in an honest manner.

Your eyes may be opened if you ask the children about how they're being acknowledged at school for demonstrating good character, and how their peers perceive the honour. Dylan, an 11-year-old grade 6 student in Ontario, says that one of the ways in which his school identifies and awards students is by calling out their names at character assemblies and giving them certificates. However, he is sometimes confused by the discrepancy between what the teachers say about the trait and the student to whom they have chosen to award the certificate. When students get awards for modelling the trait, says Dylan, "the teachers don't even say why the kid deserves the award." His feeling is that the most deserving student does not always receive the award. He's convinced that his teacher just looks through the list of students in the class when she's asked to make a selection. "One time there was this bully in our class that she gave the respect award to. That time, especially, I think that my teacher just picked a random name because I definitely don't think he deserved it."

As well as asking questions, attend character-based assemblies as often as you can. I'm sure you will learn a lot by doing so.

However, character education is so much more than assemblies and completing worksheets with sentences beginning, "Courage is . . ." or "I showed initiative when . . ." If we don't authentically model what we want and help our children to experience the attributes we are trying to instil, our words and definitions are empty.

Character education is not about *telling* our children to be more responsible with chores, *telling* them to persevere with their homework when they want to walk away, or *insisting* that they tell the truth no matter what. It is about *showing* our children how to persevere, be responsible, and be honest.

Once families have developed a common language for communicating about character, parents and children can partner more effectively. When my then 17-year-old daughter went back on her word by not wanting to clean up after dinner, I said, "I feel that you are being disrespectful. You are going against something that we had all agreed on."

The agreed-upon guidelines had come about as a result of chatting with public school administrator Arthur Birenbaum about the Touchstone project[1] he developed and implemented at a school he was teaching at a few years ago. Following our chat, I realized that a Family Touchstone would be another great way for us, as a family, to come together to determine our values and beliefs. A way for us to create phrases that embodied what was important to us; a document for us to refer back to. So, during a family meeting, we completed sentences such as "In this family, we will . . ." And "In this family, we will not stand for . . ." Our resulting sentences included "In this family we will share our belongings and our chores," and "In this family we will not stand for being yelled or sworn at by one another." Once our Touchstone was written up, we posted it on the fridge door. This reminded us of what we had agreed upon. We had created a common language. Then, when my daughter wanted to go back on her word, I pointed to our Touchstone and reminded her of what we had agreed upon.

When a parent recently told me that he and his wife felt "lucky" that their 17- and 19-year-old sons still enjoyed going on camping trips with them, I reminded him that luck was only a small part of why his sons wanted to hang with them. I proposed that along with a certain amount of luck, there was likely a great deal of time spent in creating an environment of mutual respect, and also probably a lot of effort put into making their time together interesting and fun.

Teaming up with our children requires taking an active interest in what is going on in their lives, talking to them about issues that pertain to character (such as bullying and honesty), and including the ten crucial characteristics in your mutual vocabulary of words. When I think back to my personal dictionary of words when I was growing up, I realize that I would never have had words such as initiative, integrity, and empathy on my list, let alone knowing their meaning and using them in the proper context. Chloe not only knows what they mean but I hear her, and her peers, using them appropriately all the time.

Partnering with your children also means keeping your eyes and mind open to recognizing when they are not displaying the characteristics you had hoped for, and looking for the cause. Sometimes difficult behaviour may not be a reflection of your character *or* theirs. And the real cause has to be indentified before character modelling can succeed. Consider the following story.

Years ago, the mother of a four-year-old scheduled an appointment to speak to me about her son's aggressive and impulsive behaviour. She had previously seen another therapist but wanted a second opinion after becoming frightened about the long-term consequences of her son's behaviour. Apparently, after she described some of these behaviours, such as using their budgie as a puck while playing indoor hockey, the therapist had said that her son's apparent lack of empathy towards living things was a red flag. She told the already fearful mom that suicide bombers, for example, lacked empathy. Petrified that her son was going to grow up wanting to kill others, she brought him to see me. She was worried that despite her best intentions, she could do nothing to change his destiny. After following up on my referral for an assessment, her son was diagnosed with Attention Deficit

Hyperactivity Disorder and prescribed medication. Months later, with the right medication and his parents' continued support and patience, she noted a complete change in his behaviour. A couple of years have passed since I saw them last. Recently, she called to share that her son had received that month's empathy award at school. Teachers have commented on how empathic he is towards his peers, and how he is especially responsive to the children with special needs who spend some time in their classroom.

When Children Become Models: Jordana's Story

Sometimes your effort to foster character in your kids will receive a very special reward, when you find yourself being enthralled as your own child leads *you* on a character journey. That is what happened to Canadian parents Julie and Eric Weiss. Their story also demonstrates the enormous power of *noticing* and *encouraging* character attributes in your children.

The Weisses have three grown children. When their eldest child, Jordana, was nine years old, Julie found out that Free The Children, the world's largest network of children helping children through education, was running a summer camp around social action and social issues. Julie says that Jordana was not the kind of kid that loved sports or particularly wanted to go to a sleepover camp. However, when Julie saw a little ad for the camp, she intuitively felt that it was something Jordana might like. Julie knew that Jordana was bright and interested in causes. She would always speak up. "I thought that this would be a constructive way to use her natural skills—it just seemed like a fit for her," says Julie. "So I asked her to try the day camp for two weeks and promised that if she didn't like it, she didn't have to go back."

Jordana was the youngest camper and this appealed to her, being the eldest child in their family. She also really enjoyed the kind of people the camp was attracting—laid back but also very compassionate. Julie says that Jordana had never cared about what she wore or what other people thought. "She was really lucky to find people who accepted her for who she was and whose values were similar to hers. They were 'authentic' people—a word that Jordana used even at a young age," says Julie.

At the end of the first week of camp, the organizers invited Jordana to attend an overnight leadership training program for a week. She immediately said yes, despite never having gone to an overnight camp. Julie drove Jordana to York University's Glendon campus in Toronto and dropped her off. She had just celebrated her tenth birthday. Julie remembers driving away and thinking, "Oh my God, am I insane?" So she turned her car around and went back. By the time she returned, Jordana had been "swallowed up into the group and she was fine" and so Julie left once again. "She was so young," says Julie: she had even taken her blankie with her. Despite Julie's apprehension, Jordana loved every moment.

After that, Jordana became very involved with Free The Children. She went to weekly meetings during the school year, was on their board of directors, and began organizing her own campaigns. Amazingly, she began travelling with Free The Children to countries such as Mexico, Ecuador, India, and Nicaragua when she was very young—around 12 years old. It started this way: for her Bat Mitzvah, she asked guests to make donations instead of giving her gifts. Her mom says that on her invitation was written, "I have everything I want and need, but I would love it if you could make a donation to build a school in a developing country." Most people did as asked and Jordana raised money, but not quite enough to build a school. Then the Weisses heard about another family who were also trying to raise money to build a school in an underprivileged country. Their daughter Emma, who would have been the same age as Jordana, had tragically drowned the summer before. Emma had heard about Free The Children and her dream too had been to build a school. At her funeral, in lieu of flowers, her parents asked for donations to help build a school.

The two families pooled their money so that a new school could be built in Ecuador. That summer, Jordana travelled to Ecuador and rode up into the mountains for two days on the back of a mule so that she could bring a photograph of Emma to the new school that was named in her honour.

The snowball effect of Jordana's passion eventually spread to the rest of her family. As Julie watched Jordana's growing involvement from the sidelines, she realized what a great group of people Jordana was working with. She was inspired to start volunteering her time. Eventually, it became "a real family thing." Her other children joined her when it was time to pack school kits to send to Sierra Leone or Kenya or Nicaragua, and they too learned about banding together to help others in need. Their son, Jesse, travelled to Mexico and Kenya at the age of 13 to build schools and has continued to volunteer his time for great causes. Rachel, their youngest, attended the Free The Children leadership academy in Toronto during the summer of 2008.

Julie says that they keep a big map of the world on their kitchen wall. Over the years, they've met a lot of people through Free The Children and had many kids from different countries stay in their home. Her children have a whole system of little pins—they mark places where they know people. And now with the internet, they can stay in touch. When they hear about something that has happened in Kenya, for example, they experience it a little differently than other children, or adults, might.

So what's the secret? "It's about really listening to your kids, what they want to do and what they're interested in," Julie says. "Jordana's interests took us, as a family, on a certain journey. The people that this brought into our lives have enriched everybody in the family. Our kids have also learned that everybody can do their little bit."

But there's another side too. When I spoke to Jordana to hear her perspective, she talked about all the people who have had a positive influence in her life. She says that she was raised in an environment where there were always newspapers around. She and her siblings were encouraged to read them and to watch the news. "It was an environment of lifelong education and becoming more aware and open to your surroundings," she says. "Even now my dad will call me to talk about quotes he reads in the newspaper—quotes about things that I am interested in. He tries to engage with me about politics and world affairs. Dad is quieter than Mom," she says. "More the behind-the-scenes person. When Free The Children moved offices, he helped to pack their stuff and helped them move. He's quite practical. My mom provides us with more emotional support."

Her definition of a parent who models with intention is "someone that your kids and other people in the community can look up to." She says that her parents have definitely been models to her in that they have always shown her how one should behave as an adult in the community. Although Jordana may be a few years—at least—away from having children of her own, she is quite sure that she would like to follow in her parents' footsteps.

Short & Sweet

- As we continue to develop character in our children, acknowledging the progress that we see is critically important. Also, helping them to become more aware of the process through which they are developing character is invaluable.
- Teaming up with our children requires taking an active interest in what is going on in their lives, talking to them about

issues that pertain to character (such as bullying and honesty), and including the ten crucial characteristics in your mutual vocabulary of words.

- Sometimes your effort to foster character in your kids will receive a very special reward, when you find yourself being enthralled as your own child leads *you* on a character journey.

Chapter 7

Joining Forces with Educators

"The collaboration between home and school has the potential to make a really big difference."
—Thomas Lickona, in conversation, 2008

Even before today's character education movement, children absorbed a lot about values from their time at school. It wasn't just about reading, writing, and arithmetic. Completing homework assignments and mastering the curriculum were the academic benefits, but there were others too.

Robert Fulghum, author of *All I Really Need to Know I Learned in Kindergarten*, writes, "All I really need to know about how to live and what to do and how to be I learned in kindergarten. Wisdom was not at the top of the graduate-school mountain, but there in the sand pile at Sunday School." He lists some of the things he learned: "Share everything, play fair, don't hit people, put things back where you found them, and clean up your own mess."

Now, with the advent of explicit character education, children get an organized, consistent package to ensure that they don't pick up these life skills haphazardly, but in a way that is carefully planned out and executed. As the movement takes hold around the world, more and more students are gaining principles that will stand them in good stead for the rest of their lives.

So schools have a lot to give. But even educators at the forefront of character education agree that what children learn at home is primary. As Thomas Lickona writes, "The family is the first school of virtue. It is where we learn about love. It is where we learn about commitment, sacrifice, and faith in something larger than ourselves. The family lays down the moral foundation on which all other social institutions build."[1] An article by Marvin Berkowitz and Melinda Bier* concurs: "Although school has a central role in developing students' character, the most profound impact on students' development comes from their families, notably their parents—whether we look at social, moral, behavioural, or academic development."[2]

Long before our children become part of a formal education program, parents can begin modelling character. But once you've got the warm hearth of values glowing at home, once your own modelling is well under way with the partnership of your spouse and your children, you can turn the flame up even higher if you look for ways to partner with your child's school.

What the schools are trying to do has a better chance of succeeding if they enjoy the active partnership of parents. In their 2005 "Character Education" article, Berkowitz and Bier talk about a study by Henderson and Berla** (1994) which concludes, "The single best predictor of student success in school is the level of parent involvement in a child's education." The study further underscores how important it is for school administrators and teachers to integrate and involve parents in the development of character education programs in the school. It advises that

* Bier is a Research Scientist at the Center for Character and Citizenship at the University of Missouri-St. Louis.

** Anne Henderson and Nancy Berla are well known for their research on the impact of the involvement of parents and families in the schooling of their children.

schools "build partnerships with as many parents as possible so that parents are collaborators" in the design, delivery, and evaluation of character education curriculum.

What can you, as a parent, do to contribute to building this bridge?

First, be curious. Take an active interest in what is happening on the education front. Is there a program for character education offered at your child's school and what is it? What formal training have the teachers received around character education? Second, look for a role you can play in the school's program or how you can contribute towards starting one. Third, try to coordinate what you are modelling at home with what the school is doing.

Let's look at these steps in more detail. Do you know if your child's school has woven a character development program into its academic curriculum? If so, do you know *how* character education is being integrated? What formal training have the teachers received and what is planned for the future? Education leader Dr. Merle Schwartz* says there is a "huge dark hole" that needs to be filled with teachers who graduate from teacher education programs with knowledge about how to integrate character development into the curriculum and how to model behaviour consistent with what they are teaching. She says that in the United States, only 13% of teacher education programs are meeting this need.

Most importantly, do you feel included? Can you find opportunities to become more involved? You may have read a large sign outside of the school announcing the character attribute of the month or something about character in your child's school newsletter; you may have attended a "character" assembly (sometimes without being informed that the certificates the children receive

* Dr. Merle Schwartz has a doctorate in education, is a former special education teacher and school psychologist, was Director of Education and Research at the Character Education Partnership based in Washington, D.C., and is now an independent learning consultant.

are under the character education umbrella). Do you know how you can work as a partner in making sure that the messages at school are reinforced and supplemented at home, and vice versa?

Although schools may have seen great success with the implementation of character education programs and noted the benefits for both students and staff, I believe that some may not have adequately equipped parents with the resources and information necessary to bridge the gap between home and school.

Like most parents you are probably good at keeping track of when to attend parent-teacher and school council meetings and when to volunteer at pizza days and on school trips. Of course, your continued involvement goes a long way. Getting to know your child's teachers and the principal adds to the creation of a cohesive "home away from home." When it comes to character education, your role is perhaps even more essential.

As I've said before, it's not the case that parents are the "supporting actors" in a production where educators are the leads. If anyone is primary in the formation of children of good character, parents are. Like most forms of partnership, however, this is win-win. Schools benefit from parents' whole-hearted participation in character building, and parents benefit from the contributions of schools. In fact that isn't quite right: it is children who benefit most from both.

Partnering with Your Child's Teachers

If you were asked to reflect upon your school days, I'm sure that you would remember a special relationship with one or more of your teachers. A friend once shared with me that her grade three teacher, second to her mother, was one of the most important people in her life. "This special teacher showed me the path of righteousness and wisdom," she said.

When your child is in kindergarten, it seems easier to get to know his teacher. As our children grow older, and especially when they are in high school, parents pull back—partly because they don't feel as needed and partly because their presence may be more of an embarrassment than a joy to their child. However, just because you no longer go on field trips with your 13-year-old, don't think that there aren't ample opportunities for connecting with his teacher while still respecting your teen's need for greater autonomy.

My husband and I look forward to parent-teacher interviews. We still very much enjoy meeting our 16-year-old's teachers and putting a face to the person we've heard stories about. Although I often hear parents saying that high school teachers don't really want to be bothered with parents of students who are doing well, we have always felt welcomed by our children's teachers and we always come away from the meetings learning something new.

Talking from the other side of the fence, educator Lynn Wilson* believes that it is part of a teacher's responsibility to develop strong reciprocal relationships with his or her students' family and the community in which the family lives. Often, the teacher becomes part of the extended family in support of the child. She says that teachers should not see their students in isolation and believes that it is crucial to look at the whole family—siblings, parents, even grandparents. "Today's families are far more complicated," she says. "I've had family/teacher interviews with 12 people sitting at the table."

Although your children may resist your involvement at first, it is important that they understand your goal of partnering with the very people who are playing a crucial role in helping to shape them. In order for children to thrive in their learning

* Lynn Wilson began her career in primary schools, then a co-operative, nursery schools and, for over 20 years, was on faculty in the School of Early Childhood at George Brown College in Toronto. She has also written a textbook entitled *Partnerships: Families and Communities in Early Childhood Development*, 4th Edition, Nelson Education, Canada, 2010.

environment, they need to feel the strength, support, and guidance of the most important adults in their lives, working as a team.

Walk the Walk, Don't Just Talk the Talk

How well does your child's teacher model good character? How is good character modelled by other staff members and the principal?

Schwartz, whose dissertation was on modelling behaviour by teachers, believes that as long as teachers' perspective is that character education is what you *do* to kids, then they discount their own role. Teachers can be much more effective if they are really conscious of what their own behaviour models and deliberate in helping kids understand *what* they're modelling—that is, "actually vocalizing what they're doing when they're doing it." In her published research, Schwartz found that the messages that teachers thought their students were receiving by way of modelling versus what the kids were actually picking up were only in alignment about 33% of the time.[3] She says that teachers need to dialogue with their students about this. She recommends that teachers hold regular class meetings so that teacher and students can provide feedback to one another. The teacher may give her students an example of when they modelled a specific character trait really well and then ask them to provide feedback about a time when she modelled well and a time when she may not have. This is similar to what I will suggest in the next chapter, "Family as a Foundation," where parents are encouraged to give and receive feedback from their children at home.

Kelly Fassel, former principal of our local public school, had a good story about how much more effective *modelling* is than *telling* students what to do. She shared with me the story of how some of the younger students at school began volunteering their time to help maintain the school's property. It began during lunch recess one day when she came out with a bag and gloves and started picking up garbage on her own. Very soon, she says, there were kids running up to her with paper and litter in their hands, wanting to put it into her garbage bag. The next day they asked if they could have their own bags and gloves and it just blossomed from there. Eventually she even gave them a name—"the garbage busters." They became volunteers throughout the year and a formal schedule was created. Amazingly, some kids were disappointed if their names didn't appear on the schedule for any given week.

As you become more involved in partnering with your child's teacher, you may get reinforcement from one another, and share insights.

Birenbaum, now public school administrator and father to two teenaged boys, has been in the field for more than 25 years. A former teacher, he feels strongly about providing students with an understanding of what character means—what the behavioural traits are and how to interact with one another appropriately. He believes, "You actually have to model what it is you expect the children to do. As the saying goes, it isn't enough to talk the talk: you have to walk the walk too."

Birenbaum recognizes that principals and teachers, like parents, do not always set a good example. He told me, "As a teacher, you can't say, 'This is what responsibility means, kids,' but then not have a test marked when you said you would or forget to bring something in that you promised you would." The lesson for teachers and parents: part of modelling a principle is to avoid blatantly violating it.

Birenbaum offered other examples: he has noticed that some teachers stand silently and respectfully alongside the students while the national anthem is playing during the morning announcements, whereas others continue marking or checking off attendance at their desks. He notices teachers talking to one another on the sidelines during assemblies and then reprimanding their students for doing just that. "How can we expect the children to know that they're supposed to stand in respect for the national anthem if we don't?" he asks. "How can we ask kids not to chew gum in class or not to talk to one another during assemblies if they see us doing just that?" Teachers are no more immune to these slip-ups than are parents.

After attending a character symposium in Washington in 2008, Birenbaum reported that although we have a few teachers in every school who are committed to character education, many teachers still say that they don't have time for it and don't want to take on anything more. This upsets him. "I don't know how much time it takes to stand at the door and say good morning to the children when they walk in. Sometimes that's all you need to make a child feel like he belongs and counts. And once children feel that they belong and count, their behaviour adjusts accordingly," he says. By taking the time to model good character, Birenbaum believes that teachers, like parents, can cut down on the time that will otherwise be needed to deal with difficult behaviours. If children are treated respectfully, fairly, and with honesty, they are going to perform better academically and behave better at school and home.

Birenbaum admits that trying to fully engage his colleagues can "sometimes feel like an uphill battle." He has learned that "you can't go up to teachers who are professionals and say, this is how I want you to behave." If he models without preaching, his colleagues, just like his students, are more likely to follow his good example. "I really believe," he says, "that the staff at school sense my commitment. Just as some teachers are passionate about math education or literacy, when they see my passion, what I am doing, and the success that I am having with students' positive behaviour, they are more likely to think—well, maybe I'll try that too."

In a similar way, I believe that if you, as a parent, continue to model positive attributes and see changes in your children's behaviour, other parents will be encouraged to share this way of life.

Good modelling is contagious.

When a parent and teacher partner, there is more consistency and less chance that a child will lose his or her way. A child who sees that his teacher has expectations that have not been established at home has an opening for evasion. For example, if a child is not taught responsibility at home in the form of hanging up his coat, making his bed, or putting his clothes in the laundry hamper, it may be difficult for a teacher to get him to take responsibility at school. That child may leave his textbooks in his desk at school instead of taking them home to complete homework, or may routinely lose pieces of clothing at school. On the other hand, a child who follows family rules only because she is afraid of what her parent might do if she resists may render powerless a teacher who tries to change certain behaviours by employing a more reasoned approach. Similarly, if a parent does not model and encourage respect towards others (if, for example, she tolerates being spoken to rudely or acts that way towards her child), then the child may show disrespect at school by interrupting the teacher or not following the rules of the classroom.

It is helpful for parents to understand the school's philosophy on teaching values, and to make sure that approach is in keeping with what he or she thinks is appropriate at home. For example, if your child's school does not encourage students to speak up or to state strong opinions and you do (so long as it is respectful), there may be a mismatch. If the gap between what the school believes and what the parent believes is too wide, the child will likely fall through it. Let's say the school policy is that a child who "answers back" should be given a detention. If the parent does not believe that this models fairness and tells his or her child so, then the child is more likely to defy the school's reaction and to keep on stating his opinion openly.

In cases of serious disagreement over a school policy issue, the parent should talk to the school administrator or principal to voice his or her concerns and try to find a way to be on the same page.

As a way of truly working together, it would be wonderful if schools could arrange for interested parents to attend professional development days, so that they can learn alongside the teachers regarding the development of character programs in the school or anything that has to do with the general tone of the school (i.e., that which is not related to academics *per se*).

At parent-teacher interviews, instead of only focusing on academic strengths and weaknesses or going over the most recent report card, the teacher and parents may want to look at the child as a whole and discuss other aspects of his or her character. For example, they might share examples of how the child shows responsibility or empathy at home and in the classroom. Then they could share this information with the child in an informal or written manner, so that the child would feel that teacher and parent are working as partners on the development of his character—partners with consistent viewpoints.

Another way in which parents and teachers can collaborate is at school events such as character assemblies. Perhaps parents could be advised of these assemblies well in advance and be made to feel welcome. Perhaps schools could even host some assemblies in the evening so that working parents may attend. And schools can think of ways in which a parent might get involved: at each assembly, a different parent could make a mini-presentation on the character trait of the month and how it applies in the home.

In the last three chapters we have seen that when you partner with your co-parent, your children, and their teachers, you will have greater success in developing children with character. Teamwork can sometimes be challenging but the rewards are tremendous. That will now become even clearer as we embark on the series of family meetings that I call The Family Plan, in Part Two. The purpose of The Family Plan is to take character-building to the next plateau in the family, by involving all the members as a team in an intentional, conscious enterprise fuelled by mutual feedback. The next chapter will begin that process by discussing how to achieve more time spent together as a family, and how to conduct a successful family meeting.

Short & Sweet

- With the advent of character education programs, children get an organized, consistent package to ensure that they don't pick up these life skills haphazardly but in a way that is carefully planned out and executed.
- Once your own modelling is well under way with the partnership of your spouse and your children, you can turn the flame up even higher if you look for ways to partner with your child's school.
- What the schools are trying to do has a better chance of succeeding if they enjoy the active partnership of parents. A 1994 study concluded, "The single best predictor of student success in school is the level of parent involvement in a child's education."
- What can you, as a parent, do to contribute to building a bridge between home and school?
  - First, be curious. Take an active interest in what is happening on the education front. Is there a program for character education at your child's school and what is it?
  - Second, look for what role you can play in the school's program, or how you can contribute towards starting one.
  - Third, try to coordinate what you are modelling at home with what the school is doing. When home and school send conflicting signals about values, the child can fall through the gap between them. So it's important to find ways to be on the same page.
- In order for children to thrive in their learning environment, they need to feel the strength, support, and guidance of the most important adults in their lives, working as a team.

Part Two

Chapter 8
Family as a Foundation

"If there is anything that we wish to change in the child, we should first examine it, and see whether it is not something that could better be changed in ourselves."
—C.G. Jung, *Integration of the Personality*, 1939

In Part One, we explored various aspects of modelling and teaching good character to your children, and the importance of partnering with your co-parent, your children, and your children's schools in that effort. What I want to focus on now is *your family as a unit*, and how it can become a full-fledged, mutually reinforcing character-building team, as well as a healthier, happier family, with the help of a series of planned family meetings.

In this chapter I'll start with ways of spending more quality time together as a family, and then will go on to the how-to's of the vital family meeting.

It's important to create opportunities for togetherness as a family, not just in order to enjoy each other's company—though that is incredibly worthwhile and often neglected—but also to share plans, goals, beliefs, and values with one another. When you express to each other your individual dreams and your vision for the family as a whole, you construct a solid foundation from which your family can grow.

Showing that you yourself want to spend time together with your family is itself a wonderful attribute to model to your children. Even though we sometimes prefer to read a book over playing a board game or taking a walk together, we often need to defer our personal needs for the sake of creating time for the family. When we tell our children that we have put time aside especially for them and then ask what it is that they would most like to do, we are sending a powerful message. We are suggesting that our time as a family is extremely valuable and worthy enough to put everything else aside for. If one or more of your children reject the idea of spending time together as a family, remind them how important they are and how incomplete your family feels without each of them. Ask that they honour you with at least an hour of their time just once. Then, make sure to encourage their wanting to return or stay longer by doing something that everyone will enjoy.

I often hear parents talk about how each member of the family is off doing his or her own thing, even when they are at home together. Each watching a different show on TVs in separate rooms or each on his or her computer or cellphone. It's easy for this to happen. Detachment creeps into our lives and before we know it, even meals are eaten at different times and in separate rooms. Reversing or changing this separateness is entirely possible. We need to create opportunities for connection in our families so that our children can feel worthy and significant.

While writing this book, buried deep in research notes and with thoughts of modelling foremost in my mind, I noticed that our family was too often scattered in different corners of the house. So I called a family meeting and voiced my concerns. I suggested that we implement a "no screens" policy from 6 to 8 p.m. every day. I shared my thoughts about wanting those two hours free from distractions. I shared that I was tired of having to compete with forces as powerful as the internet and television. At first, my younger daughter was furious. "You can't tell me what to do with my time!" she insisted. "You're right," I responded, "but I love spending time with you and I am requesting more of it." Once she had calmed down, she suggested that she should have a choice as to when she took her two hours of "no screens" time. Although I am all for democratic decision-making, I shared my rationale for everyone in the family having the same two hours without screens. Eventually she agreed to try it for a short period and I agreed to consider other options if it was really as intolerable as she predicted it might be.

My husband was with the children on the first night of executing the new policy. When I arrived home from the office, I found him and our younger daughter lying on one couch playing a word game and our older daughter, on the other, reading a book—a rare sight!

I congratulated them on their successful survival. After a month of implementing the new plan, we relaxed the policy to include weekdays only. Monday to Friday with no screens from 6 to 8 p.m. was more successful than even I had anticipated. Although Talia would never admit it, I think she actually enjoyed having some time away from screens. She read more books that summer than the year before, and she liked spending more time hanging out as a family. I sometimes think that my children saw this exercise as a bit of a personal challenge. It isn't easy to find ways of entertaining oneself when you've been so used to being entertained. I felt particularly proud of their perseverance, especially at the beginning when it was more difficult. I thanked them for showing respect by upholding the policy, even on evenings when my husband and I were not around to supervise them.

Unfortunately, the "no screens" policy lasted only as long as the summer holidays. Once school began, it was difficult to figure out whether their needing to be at the computer was legitimately school-related or not. With so many extracurricular activities and homework to be completed, we often find ourselves, once again, off in different corners of the house. However, I do believe that those few months of no screens did help to bring our family together. It did remind us of how much we enjoy each other's company, and we are more connected to one another than before the "no screens" summer.

How to Conduct a Family Meeting

What *has* continued is coming together as a family once a month to have a family meeting. We take turns writing down personal and family goals, request changes of one another, and determine consequences for problems that keep recurring. Writing our plans down and then looking back over them at the next meeting helps to keep each of us accountable to one another. It's also amazing what wise words we hear coming from our children. During one of our meetings, our then nine-year-old told her then 17-year-old sister, "Talia, we don't have many rules, but we do have to have boundaries." It is also amazing to watch our evolution over a series of meetings and the way in which feelings are articulated. At one meeting, the usual bickering between our girls was replaced with a mature discussion about feelings. "When you don't pay attention to what I am showing you," said our youngest to her sister, "I find that offensive."

Family meetings are a great way of laying a foundation and creating opportunities for togetherness. In the context of parents modelling character, they provide an opportunity for parents, kids, and possibly others living at home, to come together to start talking about developing a framework of goals and beliefs worthy of a family of character. Families can meet around the kitchen table, in their living room or at a restaurant (round tables are great for democratic decision-making—no one is sitting at the head), to brainstorm, record, and refine their goals and ground rules, and to engage in discussions.

Family meetings can be equally successful when conducted by a single parent and his or her only child as when two parents and several children meet. Don't dismiss the idea of a family meeting if you are a single parent with one child. Even though you may have more one-on-one time than parents with two or more children, you are still not that likely to informally discuss values or beliefs while playing in the park or eating dinner together. These discussions need to be *planned.*

The family meeting was originally called The Family Council. The idea was developed by the late Dr. Rudolf Dreikurs, an American psychiatrist and a student of eminent psychologist Alfred Adler.

American psychotherapist and author Lynn Lott writes about being introduced to the idea of family meetings in 1973 when her older child was four and her younger was two. She and her family met on and off over the next 12 years and the practice continued after her children left for college and her 16-year-old stepson moved in.

In "Family Meetings,"[1] Lott writes about their two ground rules—practising mutual respect and maintaining emotional honesty. She defines mutual respect as allowing for differences, staying away from judging another person as being right or wrong, and respecting each other's thoughts and feelings as well as one's own. She says, "We don't agree to things unless we feel we can live with them and we take care of ourselves and don't expect others to be mind readers. We see mistakes as opportunities to learn and grow and chances to try again."

She says that "emotional honesty is a skill." Feeling words such as happy, angry, irritated are used to "describe something that is going on inside of us and [provide] information about us. Feelings aren't judgements about others and are different from thoughts. Feelings aren't good or bad, right or wrong, proper or improper. Feelings aren't logical." She writes, "We cannot tell how a person is feeling just from observing their behaviour. People can smile when they feel angry, eat when they're not hungry, sleep when they're depressed, and cry from happiness. To really know someone's feelings, we must ask them or have them tell us."

The second aspect of emotional honesty focuses on the word "honest." Lott acknowledges that communicating our true feelings to others can be very frightening. "We are vulnerable, and people around us are not always well trained and sensitive to listen to feelings without taking them personally, explaining them away or correcting them. It's still worth the risk, for without emotional honesty, there is very little self-acceptance, acceptance of others, or growth."

Lott uses a phrase that is worth pausing over. She says that parents need to learn the art of "listening without fixing, criticizing, judging, or defending." This made me recall one of the first things that therapists are taught. When listening to a person's problems or troubles, most of us tend to leap immediately into problem-solving, not realizing that the person needs something else before they get to that: they need *validation*, the sense that someone else is listening to them and sees their feelings and thoughts as legitimate. As Lott says, learning this important lesson can help the family meeting become "an invaluable tool for communication, conflict resolution, joint planning, and overall good feelings."

Family meetings encourage everyone to work as a team, and they allow us to learn things that we might otherwise not know . . . like what others are thinking and feeling. Anything may get discussed, from planning a family vacation, to deciding how to take care of a sick animal to dividing household chores. Keep in mind that if you call family meetings only to preach and lay down laws, your children will not want to participate.

Family meetings work best when conducted in a democratic, respectful manner and when each person has equal time to share his or her ideas without fear of being judged, contradicted, or condemned. By "democratic" I don't mean that all decisions are decided by voting: some matters will require the parents' guidance and leadership (based on their greater knowledge and experience); but even these can leave each child feeling that his or her viewpoint was listened to in a fair way. *That* is what democratic means in this context.

Family meetings also work best when the adults in the family understand the workings of the meeting and figure out an agenda prior to sharing their ideas with their children. Once the adults have modelled chairing the meetings and setting agendas, the children can take turns leading family meetings. As well, children and adults can take turns keeping minutes that can be referred to at subsequent meetings. Mutual respect and a strong rule against ganging up against one another should be stressed. If anyone notices that there are alliances forming among members of the family, the person chairing the meeting should intervene and ask them to start over.

Key Points to Remember when Conducting a Family Meeting

These are best discussed by the adults prior to calling a family meeting and then shared with the children at the first meeting:

- Allow each person time to share his or her ideas. Don't belittle any idea, feelings, thoughts, or concerns. No idea should be viewed as unworthy.
- Allow for individual differences. Agree to disagree, if necessary. Stay away from right and wrong, blaming or criticizing.
- Include young children. Even if they aren't as verbal or as involved, let them play alongside you if necessary. Although very

young children may not be as able to make certain decisions, they can be given choices such as "Would you prefer to go out for pizza or burgers?"

- If anyone refuses to participate, share how much he or she will be missed and encourage their attendance. If they still refuse, don't force the issue. However, let them know that family decisions may be made that affect them too and that if they are not present, their voices will not be heard.

Family meetings are a way for you to come together as a team and lay a foundation for building character. The Family Plan will be implemented (as laid out in the next chapter) over four weekly meetings, and then as a series of monthly meetings, as detailed in chapters 12 to 21. These will allow your family to explore the ten crucial characteristics that help to define character.

I know that it may be difficult to hear what your children have to say about you at the family meetings, but consider the rewards of teaching them how to openly, honestly, and respectfully communicate their thoughts and observations. I often recommend that parents pretend they are listening to a friend's child rather than their own while receiving feedback. Doing so will help you get the distance you need to listen to your children without becoming defensive. If you are inviting the children to observe you while you observe them, be prepared for what they may say about what they see. I think that it takes a certain amount of confidence as a parent to be able to earnestly listen and learn from their comments. The more you practise modelling and implementing your plan, the more confident you will be, because you will have taken conscious control of the very behaviours that your children might critique.

Some parents may choose to receive feedback from their children independent of the group meeting—being criticized in front of a group can press major buttons. For example, a parent may request that his children share their observations at bedtime when they are alone. Critical feedback, at any age, can be a challenge, both to give and to receive.

Many parents share how much easier it is for family members to criticize rather than compliment each other. However, they find that when they provide *positive* feedback to one another, they encourage more of what they want to see. This is so much more successful than talking about what is wrong and expecting change after telling others that you know they can do better. The latter, in fact, can be quite discouraging. (Think of how you might feel after preparing and serving a meal, if you were told, "That was good, but I know you can do better!") Using the ten crucial characteristics as key words in your vocabulary, try to encourage each child or family member at least once a day. For example, if you notice your child working hard at a school project, don't wait until it is complete to praise the end result. Rather, encourage the process by saying something like "Wow, look at that neat printing. Your perseverance has really paid off!"

A family is like a jigsaw puzzle. Each piece corresponds to a family member and the strengths he or she possesses. Not everyone is going to share the same strengths. Not everyone is going to be prone to the same weaknesses. However, when all the pieces come together to form a whole, it couldn't be what it is without every one of them.

It is now time to embark on the four family meetings that are part of The Family Plan. This Plan will help you understand each other's points of view on character, bring you closer as a family, and meld you together as a character-building team.

Before actually holding the meetings, I recommend that you read through Chapter 9 to get a sense of the materials and topics you'll be covering, and then read Chapter 10 for candid feedback from actual families who participated in The Family Plan. You'll get a good sense of what to expect and receive confirmation that it has great rewards and can be done.

Short & Sweet

- Connecting to share individual dreams, as well as your vision for the family as a unit, is vital towards creating and maintaining a solid foundation from which your family can grow.
- Modelling the desire to spend time together as a family is a priority if we are to set a good example for our children.
- We often need to defer our personal needs for the sake of creating time for the family.
- We need to create opportunities for connection in our families so that our children can feel worthy and significant.
- It's important to come together as a family about once a month for a family meeting.
- Family meetings are a great way of laying a foundation and creating opportunities for togetherness. They provide an opportunity for parents and kids (and possibly others living at home) to come together and start talking about developing a framework of goals and beliefs worthy of a family of character.
- A family is like a jigsaw puzzle. Each piece corresponds to a family member and the strengths he or she possesses.

Chapter 9

The Family Plan

"No one plans to fail but too many people fail to plan."
—Winston Churchill

Today, I am asking you to consider a very important plan, one that will allow you to achieve great success as a family. Each person's definition of success may be different. My definitions include: Each person, child, and adult feels as important as the next, in terms of what he or she contributes and the way in which he or she is valued. And each person knows that no matter what, no matter when, each can count on the other—even at 3 a.m. Success also means that family members respect, care, listen to, and are honest with one another. And they really enjoy spending time as a group, look forward to taking vacations together, and share similar values, goals, and beliefs—especially when it comes to what family means and how to take care of themselves, their community, and the world.

Okay, I know this sounds a bit idyllic, and I won't say that your family (or mine) will always be this triumphant, but there's nothing wrong with planning for success, expecting success, and making optimistic prophecies. Even if you don't attain the pinnacle of what you had hoped for, at least you have reached for the stars and worked hard to try to make it happen.

Before embarking on this very exciting family project, I suggest that you read each chapter of the book up to this point, if you haven't already. It is especially important that you read Chapter 8, Family as a Foundation, so that you are prepared for how a family meeting is best planned and executed.

The Biggest Gift of All

If you carry out the steps I present here, then each of you—parent and child—will feel as if you have received the biggest gift of all: each other's time and attention. By the end of the first month of weekly meetings, you will feel a renewed sense of cohesion and connection as a family and have greater insight into each other's feelings and beliefs. You will also have defined common goals and will feel as if you are all walking in the same direction. The non-material gift that you hold in your hearts when the initial exercises are through is more precious than any piece of jewellery, car, or house that you own. The worksheets are keepsakes that will be treasured by you and your children (especially when they are older). They are a testament of your love and commitment to one another.

A Democratic Invitation

Before you decide on the date and time for the first meeting, remember that this is supposed to be a democratic process. Instead of *demanding* that your children be there and risking that they will oppose it because it's just another thing they are being told to do, approach them differently. You may want to say that you are reading this parenting book, and that it has motivated you to request a get-together as a family to create a plan for what is important to all of you. At first, you may hear sighs or jeers of disapproval at the sheer craziness of the idea, but plough on. Remember, this is what will help to define and shape your success—not just as a family, but as individuals who grow out of this family. Validate the laughs, sneers, and sighs with something like "Yes, I know it sounds corny but I'd like us to give it a try. Other families with kids your age have already tried it and although some didn't want to do it at first, they all enjoyed it and were glad they took part."

Reluctance Is Normal

Once you have your children's agreement, move quickly while you have their attention and interest. Discuss what works best for everyone's schedule and set up a time to meet during the week. Some families find that ending the meeting with a trip for a treat, for example, encourages participation. Although you should try not to present this treat as a bribe, a little bit of an incentive may get them on board until such time as they realize that the reward is in the process itself. If one or more of your children refuse to take part and won't budge, this is in itself a reflection of the state of your family and may suggest an even greater need for this plan.

Most children lack desire to be part of this type of meeting because they don't know what to expect or because they think that they will be lectured at or corrected. They may also be embarrassed to be spending time with their family—an unfortunate reflection of society's values. Recognize this reluctance as normal and ask for your child's co-operation for at least the first couple of sessions. So long as the meetings are conducted in the way that I suggested in Chapter 8 and make the child feel an increased sense of belonging, the likelihood of his or her continuing will be great. Also, reinforce the importance of each family member's attendance and the value of each of their contributions.

The Recipe

Prior to the first meeting, gather the following ingredients:

- A photograph of your family (that you can cut up)
- Scissors and tape or glue
- Pencils or pens and markers and crayons for the kids
- A three-ringed binder (or folder to hold notes)
- Lined and unlined paper
- Copies of the following six worksheets (most need one of each per family member):
  1. WHY CHARACTER MATTERS TO FAMILIES
  2. I BELIEVE
  3. OUR FAMILY'S CORE VALUES AND BELIEFS
  4. OBSERVING MYSELF AND OTHERS
  5. REFLECTIONS AFTER OBSERVING MYSELF AND OTHERS
  6. INDIVIDUAL AND FAMILY GOALS
     (All worksheets can be printed from www.characteristhekey.com.)
- Audio cassette recorder (optional)
- Large sheet of paper to write on, or if your child has a chalk or white board, you may want to set this up in front of the family to write ideas on
- Family members

Getting Prepped

Ask your children, or whoever is in the mood, to "design" a page to paste or place at the front of your binder. The TITLE at the top of the page should read:

OUR FAMILY'S PLAN

Or you can say "The ________'s Plan," filling in the last name of your family—whichever you prefer. The idea is that you personalize your binder or folder.

Leave space under the title for the **photograph**. Have someone in the family use the **scissors** to carefully cut the picture up, as if the pieces were part of a puzzle, and then **paste** or **tape** the puzzle pieces onto the title page, with some white space between each piece to show that it is a puzzle.

As you work together over the next four weeks and then continue to meet monthly, the following goals, at least, will be realized:

1. Your family will have **built a framework** within which to define your core values and beliefs.
2. You will have **developed a common language** when defining and using the top ten character traits—all keys to your success as a family.
3. You will have **developed skills** that allow each family member **to observe and analyze** his/her own behaviour and the behaviours of others within the family and the community.
4. You will have **examined the impact of the family's behaviour—as well as each individual member's behaviour**—on each other, the community, and the larger world.
5. You will all **feel part of a more connected, cohesive unit.** You will feel as if your family's foundation is more solid and secure and that you can **trust in and communicate with each other openly and honestly**, without fear of being judged or ridiculed.

6. You will have **established future goals** for each family member and for the group as a whole. In so doing, individual members as well as the family can strive towards increased awareness of self and changes in behaviour, if necessary. Modelling characteristics consistent with the family's core beliefs and values will ensure continued success towards becoming a family of character.

Before your first meeting, have everyone read and fill in the *WHY CHARACTER MATTERS TO FAMILIES* worksheet (printed from www.characteristhekey.com). Ask them to bring their completed sheets to the first meeting.

Worksheet #1

Why character matters to families

"If the family were a fruit, it would be an orange, a circle of sections, held together but separable—each segment distinct."

—Letty Cottin Pogrebin

Each member of your family is different. Some of you may be wider or taller than others. Some of you may have dark hair, others blond, some brown eyes, some hazel or blue. These physical attributes are visible. However, each person in your family also has attributes that are not directly visible—character traits. Though they aren't physical, people "see" them when you behave in a certain way. For example, if optimism is one of Dad's most visible character traits, people may see it in action by watching how he handles difficult situations. Not everyone is as accomplished at each trait. For example, you might have a very good track record for honesty; another family member may be good at being respectful, even when he or she feels like yelling at someone. The cut-out pieces of your family's photo, each one different in shape, size, and colour, fit together like pieces of a puzzle. In the same way, your family can come together to combine all of their strengths and to help one another.

Unfortunately, not everyone thinks about or wants to have character traits that are good. Sometimes, people think that it is cool to be bad, and that you're "square," a "nerd," or a "geek" if you do the "right" thing. In fact, some people tease others who want to be well behaved. Sometimes, people who adhere to a strong moral code are described in ways that seem negative—like "straight-laced." Sometimes, kids at school get bullied or teased for being the teacher's pet, for having homework done on time, for studying for tests, or for following rules. With all this teasing, it may be hard to stand alone and stick up for what you believe in. It may seem easier to join the not-so-good crowd. When you stick by what you believe in, even when it is difficult, you are acting with integrity.

Most adults say that even though it may have been difficult to stand apart from the crowd when they were younger, remaining true to their values and beliefs has helped them to feel proud of themselves and to be successful in life.

In order to begin to figure out whether your home is a place where good character exists, ask yourself these five questions. Then write your response under each question.

(*Continued*)

1. Do you feel bullied or teased by members of the family? If yes, when?

____

____

2. Do you feel you can trust family members not to lie or take things without asking? If not, why not?

____

____

3. Do family members walk away from challenges or from each other's problems when a task seems too big or difficult to take on? If yes, describe a time when this happened.

____

____

4. Do you feel encouraged to respectfully stand up for what you believe in or are you pressured to give in and do whatever the rest of the family is doing, even if you don't think it's right? If pressured, can you think of a time when this happened?

____

____

5. Do you feel that people in your family own up to their actions or do they try to blame others? If they try to blame others, do you remember a time when this happened?

____

____

When you come together as a family at your first family meeting, you will have a chance to share your responses with one another and to see how close you are to being a family with character. After the discussion, you will also have a much better idea of why character matters—not just in your home, but at school and work too.

Keep in mind that not everyone will agree with your answers. Some of you may think that people in your family show a lot of respect towards one another, while others may believe that this needs to be worked on. Remember that each person will perceive things differently. In fact, different answers can all be true, because each member may be treated differently by the others. There is no right or wrong answer. Each person is entitled to how he or she feels. Part of showing respect is to help each person feel that their opinion matters and that you are willing to work together as a team to make sure that everyone is respected.

The First Family Meeting

So, the big day has arrived and everyone is sitting around the kitchen table, in the living room, or wherever you have chosen. You have placed the chalkboard, whiteboard, or large piece of paper in a position so that everyone can see it. The adults in the room should have read up to and including this chapter to familiarize themselves with The Family Plan and feel knowledgeable and confident enough to embark on this meeting. (Having said this, I would never expect anyone to feel 100% ready in a new position and commend you for having the courage to facilitate this meeting.) You may decide to record the meeting so that you can listen and learn from it, following the discussion.

Be prepared for awkwardness, silliness, body language that says, "I don't really want to be here but I didn't really feel that I had a choice." Gradually, as the exercise unfolds, family members will relax and open up. You will notice that their body language invites increased communication. So long as you continue to encourage and show appreciation for everyone's involvement, they will continue to grow with you. At first you may feel uncomfortable when phrasing compliments in ways that seem unnatural. Rest assured that your words will come across as genuine and you will learn to feel more comfortable with this new language.

Why Character Matters

Make sure that everyone has brought their completed *WHY CHARACTER MATTERS TO FAMILIES* worksheet to this meeting. Before facilitating the sharing of responses, please read the paragraphs below. You do not necessarily need to read them out loud to your children, but during your discussion as a family you can use them as a guide towards understanding what the responses indicate about where your family stands in regard to showing character. Remember to discuss specific examples of when family members showed or did not show character towards each other.

> **Question #1: Do you feel bullied or teased by members of the family? If yes, when?**
>
> If the answers are mostly "no," then it is likely that most people in your home are showing empathy by not hurting each other's feelings and are showing respect by talking to each other in a considerate way. If the answers are mostly "yes," then your family may need to focus on developing greater respect and empathy towards one another.

Question #2: Do you feel that you can trust family members not to lie or take things without asking? If not, why not?
If the answers are mostly "yes," then it is likely that most people in your home are showing respect by not taking something without asking another's permission first and that people can trust each other to tell the truth. If the answers are mostly "no," then your family may need to focus on developing greater respect and being more honest with one another.

Question #3: Do family members walk away from challenges or from each other's problems when a task seems too big or difficult to take on? If yes, describe a time when this happened.
If the answers are mostly "no," then it is likely that most people in your home are not afraid to tackle difficult situations and to try to find a solution. If the answer is "yes," then your family may need to focus on developing greater strength in perseverance, courage when taking on large tasks, optimism that a solution can be found, and empathy in standing by one another.

Question #4: Do you feel encouraged to respectfully stand up for what you believe in or are you pressured to give in and do whatever the rest of the family is doing, even if you don't think it's right? If pressured, can you think of a time when this happened?
If the majority answer that family members are encouraged to stand up for what they believe in, then your home may be one in which integrity is encouraged. For example, if one member wants to become a vegetarian, a family with integrity and respect would allow that person to do what he or she feels is right, even if it goes against the habits of the rest of the meat-eating members. If family members are not respected for their individual choices around issues such as

this, then the family may need to focus on developing greater awareness in regards to being tolerant, fair, and respectful towards one another. The family may also need to look at how they value initiative and integrity.

Question #5: Do you feel that people in your family own up to their actions or do they try to blame others? If they try to blame others, do you remember a time when this happened?
If the majority answer that family members own up to their actions, then your home may be one in which responsibility is modelled and encouraged. If the majority says that family members try to blame others for what they have done wrong, then your family may need to focus on responsibility, fairness, and honesty.

Once the worksheet has been discussed, the next part of the meeting will be to go over, discuss definitions, and share examples of the top ten character traits.

The Character Traits

Look over the list of top ten character traits that follows or print the list from www.characteristhekey.com. Have an adult read the traits out loud or have family members take turns reading while the others listen.

Top Ten Character Traits (in random order)

RESPECT
HONESTY
FAIRNESS
COURAGE
OPTIMISM
RESPONSIBILITY
EMPATHY
INITIATIVE
PERSEVERANCE
INTEGRITY

Once you have read the ten attributes aloud, you may read the definitions and examples that follow to further illustrate what each word means. You may choose to skip the definitions and read the examples only if children show signs of becoming bored and inattentive.

Also, if there are any other character attributes that you think are important for your family, this would be the time to add them to the list and craft a good definition and example for each.

Definitions & Examples

Respect

Showing proper regard or concern for a person or thing.

She showed respect for the others by leaving the bathroom exactly the way that she found it and by not using up all the hot water in the shower in the morning.

Responsibility

The quality of being able to be trusted or depended upon when one has accepted tasks, duties, or obligations.

He showed responsibility by remembering to take home the right textbook so that he could complete his homework.

Honesty

Telling the truth; not taking what is not one's own.

She showed honesty when she volunteered that she was the one who had broken the cookie jar.

Empathy

The quality of caring about and entering into what someone else is going through and feeling.

She showed empathy when she cried after her friend's dog died.

Fairness
Applying the same standard to everyone, not being biased.
She showed fairness when she divided the pizza and gave everyone an equal number of pieces.

Initiative
The quality of making the first move when something needs to be done.
He showed initiative by offering to set the table before he was even asked.

Courage
The quality of not running away from dangerous or scary things; acting in spite of fear; bravery.
She showed courage by agreeing to go to the hospital to have her tonsils removed, even though she was afraid.

Perseverance
Persisting and carrying on with a plan, even when obstacles are encountered.
He showed perseverance by continuing up the mountain even though it was raining.

Optimism
Taking a positive attitude, anticipating a good outcome even when things look dark.
She showed optimism by focusing on getting well when she came down with a cold.

Integrity
Being true to your own beliefs and principles even when it is hard or inconvenient.
He showed integrity by sticking to his beliefs about not smoking and drinking even though many of his friends did.

Once you have read my examples out loud, you can invite those present to write down and share other examples to illustrate what each trait means. For children who cannot yet write, suggest that they draw a picture related to one or more of the attributes.

Even young children can try to complete the exercises on their own or with your help. Very young children, even those who are not yet verbal, should be made to feel as if they are an important part of the family just by being present—even if they are only playing with a puzzle or toy nearby.

In addition, your family may enjoy playing charades and guessing from each other's actions which trait they are acting out.

Wrap-up and Homework

At the end of the first session, talk to the family about setting up a time to meet again, approximately one week later. The meeting should not end until there is a consensus about the time and date. Before thanking everyone for proving their commitment to each other by being present, gather everyone's notes and place them in the binder. Then, ask each family member to take a half hour over the next day or two to complete the *I BELIEVE* worksheet (printed from www.characteristhekey.com).

Worksheet #2

I believe

The top ten character traits (in random order):

Respect	Responsibility
Honesty	Empathy
Fairness	Initiative
Courage	Integrity
Perseverance	Optimism

(*Continued*)

Complete this worksheet by first choosing one trait from the list above, and then finishing the sentences with specific examples. Bring this worksheet to the second family meeting.

1. I believe it is important to treat myself with ____.

I show this by __________________________________.

Example: I think it is important to treat myself with ***respect.***
I show this by **not eating foods that make me feel unhealthy.**

2. I believe it is important to show _______________ towards members of my family.
I do this by ______________________________________.

Example: I believe it is important to show ***respect*** towards members of my family.
I do this by **not interrupting when others are talking.**

3. I believe it is important to show _______________ towards my friends/co-workers.
I do this by ______________________________________.

Example: I believe it is important to show ***fairness*** towards my **friends**/co-workers.
I do this by **making sure that I don't hog the chip bowl and that everyone gets some.**

4. I believe it is important to show ____________ when I am around neighbours, people in our community, or any other place in the world.
I do this by ______________________________.

Example: I believe it is important to show ***empathy*** when I am around neighbours, people in our community, or any other place in the world.
I do this by **raking my elderly neighbour's grass and by giving money to a homeless person.**

5. I believe it is important to show ___________ towards our planet and the environment.
I do this by ______________________________.

Example: I believe it is important to show ***responsibility*** towards our planet and the environment.
I do this by **picking up litter on the side of the road, recycling, and not throwing litter out of the car window.**

The Second Family Meeting

Begin your second family meeting by asking each person to share their responses to the *I BELIEVE* worksheet. Again, make sure that no one is put down or ridiculed but that each idea is given equal weight and that each person is treated with respect.

As ideas are shared, record some of the key words on a larger piece of paper or a chalk or white board. Make sure that you understand the importance of welcoming each idea regardless of whether or not you feel it has merit. The way in which you model responsiveness to ideas is very important.

Once you have spent 15 or 20 minutes on this task, work together as a team to reach consensus as to which three attributes the family holds in the highest regard. Then, fill in the blanks on *OUR FAMILY'S CORE VALUES AND BELIEFS* worksheet below (printed from www.characteristhekey.com).

Worksheet #3

Our family's core values and beliefs

Complete the following statements together as a family:

1. We believe that it is important to be 1) ______________ 2) ____________________ and 3) ______________________ around our family members and others.

Example: We believe that it is important to be 1) ***Respectful*** 2) ***Honest*** and 3) ***to act with integrity*** around our family members and others.

2. Other attributes we think are equally important include: ______________________________________

Example: Other attributes we think are equally important include: ***generosity, a sense of humour, patience, flexibility,*** and ***loyalty.***

3. We believe that all of these attributes are important because: ______________________________ ____

Example: We believe that all of these attributes are important because ***they help us get along as a family and with friends.***

You are now ready to move on to the next part of this meeting . . .

Acknowledging Strengths in One Another

"Children have more need of models than of critics."

—Carolyn Coats, author of *Things Your Dad Always Told You, But You Didn't Want to Hear*

Too often we notice that a sister, brother, parent, or child is particularly good at showing empathy, is exceedingly honest, is extremely fair, or shows a great deal of integrity, but we don't mention what we are observing out loud. You may have noticed that your children seem far more comfortable with being sarcastic or insulting one another. Giving compliments often feels more awkward than offering "constructive criticism." However, when we share the good that we see, we let our children or our partner know that we have recognized their strengths. Also, by acknowledging that each person brings *different* strengths to the family unit, we can learn from one another and work as a team.

Time to Compliment

During the second family meeting, ask each family member to compliment the others by acknowledging those attributes that they show the greatest strength in.

(*Continued*)

If you're on a roll, and you want to mention more than one per family member, go for it.

When offering the compliment, ask the speaker to look directly at the family member they are talking to, and to formulate the sentence in the following manner:

"I think that ______________ shows ______________ by ______________."

Example: I think that ***Tyla*** shows ***initiative and respect towards her fish*** by ***cleaning their tank every week without being asked.***

Following this exercise, ask each person what it felt like to be acknowledged.

Wrap-up and Homework

Conclude the session by talking as a family about what it is to "observe." You may want to say something like "Observing is when we watch another's behaviour."

Hand out the *OBSERVING MYSELF AND OTHERS* worksheet and example sheet as well as the *REFLECTIONS AFTER OBSERVING MYSELF AND OTHERS* worksheet (all can be printed from www.characteristhekey.com). Ask your families members to complete both of the worksheets before the next family meeting, and set up a time to meet again, approximately one week later. You may again choose to end this meeting with a special outing, by watching a movie at home, or by playing a board game together. Before you do this, gather up all of the completed sheets (make sure that names and dates are on each) and put them into the binder.

Worksheet #4

Observing myself and others

Fill in the following table and bring your completed worksheet to your third family meeting.

Behaviour	Showed	Did not show
	+	–
RESPECT:		
RESPONSIBILITY:		
HONESTY:		
EMPATHY:		
FAIRNESS:		
INITIATIVE:		
COURAGE:		
PERSEVERANCE:		
OPTIMISM:		
INTEGRITY:		

Example: For the purpose of illustrating this exercise, I drew from the real-life examples of the children and adults who participated in the original Family Plan. Though I have filled in the entire sheet, your family members will fill in just the blanks they have observations for.

Once you have recorded some behaviours—either positive, negative, or both, complete the *REFLECTIONS AFTER OBSERVING MYSELF AND OTHERS* worksheet.

(*Continued*)

Example Sheet

Attribute	Showed (+)	Did not show (–)
RESPECT:	"I offered my seat to an elderly lady who was standing in the bus." (a thoughtful teen, aged 15)	"A friend of mine hung up on his mother in the middle of their phone conversation." (a surprised friend, aged 12)
RESPONSIBILITY:	"Mark called, as I had asked him to, to say that he had arrived home from school safely." (a relieved dad)	"Susan left the front door unlocked when she left to go to school." (a worried mom)
HONESTY:	"Laura confessed that she had taken the whole bag of cookies to her room." (a proud sister)	"I was upset when my husband showed pride in our son when he told us that he had lied about his age to save money at the movie." (a disappointed mom)

EMPATHY:	"It felt good when my sister gave me a massage after I told her that my back was hurting." (a relaxed brother, aged 9)	"When I told Mom that I wasn't feeling well, she said, 'You'll live.'" (a hurt son, aged 13)
FAIRNESS:	"When I saw that there was only one blue freezie left and that both my sister and I wanted it, I cut it in half for us to share." (a considerate sister, aged 17)	"I've noticed that our son's hockey coach, who has his son on the team, often favours his son's friends." (a disturbed dad)
INITIATIVE:	"Maddie began setting the table without my asking her to."(a pleased mom)	"We need to keep reminding Jacob to prepare his resumé so that he can look for a summer job." (a frustrated dad)

(*Continued*)

COURAGE:	"I took the training wheels off my bicycle today." (a proud daughter, aged 8)	"I didn't have the guts to tell my boss how he made me feel when he reprimanded me in front of my co-workers." (a timid dad)
PERSEVERANCE:	"My mom kept trying until we found a parking spot near the theatre." (an appreciative daughter, aged 15)	"The math was too hard for me to complete so I gave up and went outside to play." (a discouraged son, aged 10)
OPTIMISM:	"Even though it was gloomy outside, my mother-in-law said, 'This weather is bound to improve.'" (a devoted daughter-in-law)	"My brother says it always rains on his birthday." (a sad sister, aged 7)
INTEGRITY:	"Even though my friends smoke pot, I don't." (an independent teen, aged 14)	"Even though we talk about the boss behind his back, we pretend that we like him when he's around." (a disgruntled dad)

Worksheet #5

Reflections after observing myself and others

Finish the following statements and bring your completed worksheet to your third family meeting.

1. By observing my family members, I have learned that

____

____

Example: By observing my family members, I have learned that **we mostly really care about one another but don't always show it. We also yell at each other a lot and show disrespect by interrupting one another and calling each other's ideas stupid**.

2. Based on what I have seen, I believe/do not believe that we are behaving in a way that is consistent with our values and beliefs, because

____

____

Example: Based on what I have seen, I believe/**do not believe** that we are behaving in a way that is consistent with our values and beliefs because **it seems that we do share the same values in our family but that we don't always show it. For example, even though we feel that respect is very important, we are often rude to each other. Sometimes we are actually more respectful to strangers than we are to one another!**

(*Continued*)

3. The most important thing I have learned from watching others is

____

____

Example: The most important thing I have learned from watching others is **that when people are showing negative sides of the attributes, such as disrespect or irresponsibility, their behaviour gets more attention than when they are being respectful or responsible, for example.**

4. The most important thing I have learned about myself is

____

____

Example: The most important thing I have learned about myself is **that it is sometimes difficult to keep an open mind when my children are pointing out negative behaviours to me. However, I need to keep giving them permission to do so in a respectful manner, so that I keep the lines of communication open.**

The Third Family Meeting

At this meeting, each family member will have an opportunity to share what he or she has learned as a result of completing the two homework worksheets. Begin this meeting by setting some ground rules so that this sharing of observations is done in an atmosphere of mutual respect. First, ask that anyone sharing an observation be specific about what they observed rather than judgmental. For example, note the difference between the following two statements:

"You were rude when you left home this morning. You didn't say that you were going."

"I noticed that when you left the house this morning, you did not say goodbye. This made me feel ignored, because I needed to know that you were going."

The second statement avoids blame and criticism, while still communicating a clear message. These types of statements are called "I-messages."* When constructing an I-message, which does not lay blame, do so in the following manner:

"When you (describe the behaviour without judging it), I felt (state your feeling) because (say why you felt that way without criticizing or judging)."

Example: When you didn't **call at the time you said you would**, I felt **worried** because **I didn't know how to reach you and wondered where you were.**

Setting Individual and Family Goals for the Week

After everyone has had a chance to discuss their observations and reflections and has practiced using I-messages, each family member will pick one attribute he or she wants to work on during the following week. The attribute they choose should be based on the direct feedback they have received from the family that day. No family member should decide for the other or make suggestions, unless asked. Each family member, children included, should pick their own attribute. Of course, very young children may need help. For example, if a young child were to want to work on becoming more responsible, he or she may need help in

* I-messages were presented as part of Thomas Gordon's parent training program, developed in 1962. Gordon, a graduate student of renowned psychologist Carl Rogers, decided to create a complete parenting approach built on Rogers's ideas. Gordon eventually published *Parent Effectiveness Training* in 1970.

choosing a simple task (such as making his bed every morning or preparing her cereal and milk).

Finally, the family *as a whole* will choose one attribute to focus on as a unit.

Wrap-up and Homework

Hand out the last worksheet, *INDIVIDUAL AND FAMILY GOALS*, and ask each family member to write down what action they are going to take to meet their individual and family goals. Organize a time to meet the following week. You may again choose to end this meeting by doing something special together as a family. Before you do this, gather up all of the completed sheets (make sure that names and dates are on each) and put them into the binder.

Worksheet #6

Individual and family goals

1. I have decided to work on ______________________________
______________________________ this week.
I will accomplish this by ______________________________
______________________________.

Example: I have decided to work on **being more responsible** this week. I will accomplish this by **making sure that my room is tidy before I go to bed every night.**

2. As a family, we have decided to work on ______________________________.
We will accomplish this by ______________________________
______________________________.

Example: As a family, we have decided to work on **showing more empathy towards others.** We will accomplish this by **sorting through our clothes and putting together a donation for people in need.**

The Fourth Family Meeting

For your fourth family meeting, the family will come together to discuss whether or not each individual (as well as the family as a whole) was able to achieve his or her goal—and how they went about doing it. Spend time complimenting each other's successes and talking about challenges and roadblocks you encountered on the way. Remind each other that no one is expected to be perfect, and that all through life, we learn and grow from mistakes. Also, remind each other that it's always possible to try your best, so continue to be open-minded about the impact your behaviour has on others, and continue to strive towards enhancing and enriching each other's lives.

Wrap-up

Before concluding this fundamental four-week process that seeks greater success in upholding your core values and beliefs, collect all the remaining worksheets (names and dates on top of each), and summarize where you were as a family just four weeks ago and how far you have come. Thank family members for their ongoing support and remind them how valuable and important they are. Remind them also that without each of them, a part of the puzzle would be missing. Ask each person to reflect on the changes that they believe have taken place and how they feel they have benefited by being part of this process—both as individuals and as members of the group.

Congratulations

Now that you have established a strong foundation on which your family can build, I encourage you to continue meeting once a month. Set up a meeting for the beginning of the following month when you will devote a full meeting to one of the top ten character traits.

If your children's schools subscribe to a character education program, familiarize yourselves with the schedule so that you can focus on the same attributes simultaneously at home and at school. If their schools are not offering this type of program, talk to the administrators. Ask that they read this book and become aware of the programs that have been developed in Canada, the United States, and around the world. Ask them to partner with you!

Chapter 10

Feedback from Families

"Success is a journey, not a destination."
—Ben Sweetland

Prior to writing this book, I asked seven families to share some of their precious time with me and their fellow family members. Each family was asked to implement my original version of The Family Plan and provide me with feedback. The parents ranged from 33 to 51 years of age. Their children were between the ages of four and 17. Four of the seven were two-parent families with biological children. One of the remaining three was a single-parent family with two young children, another a blended family with teenaged children, and the last a couple, each in their second marriage, were raising their only biological child and intermittently parenting the father's two teenaged children from his first marriage. The sample that I selected is, I believe, a fair representation of the diversity of families today. Their feedback was invaluable to me and I hope will be equally helpful to you, setting your mind at ease that others have made the trip successfully and that it is eminently worthwhile. Their insights and experiences are in this chapter. I suggest that you read them, then go back to Chapter 9 and begin the meetings in earnest.

The families that came on board and persevered through the original series of lengthy exercises and meetings were eager to share what they had learned at the end of the month. They helped me to tweak the exercises in Chapter 9 so as to make them more family friendly. Following their completion of the exercises, I chatted with at least one parent from each family and with many of the children. They were all a great help in figuring out what to leave in and what to take out, what interested and excited them. And they all encouraged me in my efforts. They unanimously agreed that their lives had been enriched in a very short period of time and that the exercises had allowed them to explore their values and beliefs as a family. Many parents were impressed at their children's ability to communicate their ideas and feelings, and several of the parents became much more aware of how their modelling was affecting their children's behaviour.

When the parents initially approached their children, many (especially those who were 12 and older) were not very interested in taking part. When the parents explained that they were helping me with a very important project, and impressed upon them how significant their input would be, they agreed to take part—some more reluctantly than others. After four weekly meetings, every parent reported success in different forms. Those with teenagers were particularly impressed at how their children had taken to the exercises once they "got into it," and how they had communicated their feelings, "despite their silliness at times."

It was exciting for me to receive so much positive feedback. Although many of the older children were initially reluctant to engage in what they thought might be "touchy feely exercises," their feedback was extremely positive. One 15-year-old asked his parents if they could continue to meet weekly. He was relieved at being given permission to share his feelings so freely. He said that he had been fearful of doing so before, and was glad to learn new ways to communicate negative feelings respectfully. I was blown away at the perseverance that all of the children showed in working through especially arduous parts of the project (which have been condensed or eliminated as a result of their feedback), the honesty and courage that they showed in sharing their true feelings, and the empathy and respect they showed towards me in working hard at a project they knew was an important part of my research for this book.

Feedback from the seven families who took part, as well as my own, allowed me to see the merits and challenges of The Family Plan from many different angles.

Jennifer and Alan:* Reminders and Explanations, Unresolved Issues, and Becoming More Aware

Reminders and Explanations

Jennifer, married and mom to two children aged 10 and 7, said that when she approached her family with the idea of meeting to discuss good character, they all showed interest and excitement. "They are right into family meetings, so this was not difficult for me to sell," she said.

Even though they are familiar with family meetings, Jennifer said that she needed to remind her 10-year-old, Anthony, about being respectful and not laying blame during the feedback sessions. Using her skills as a life coach, she suggested that he instead offer the information in a way that helped family members understand his point of view and encouraged *them* to decide if they wanted to make improvements. She was glad to see that he was able to independently offer feedback in a different manner following her reminders.

* The majority of names of participants throughout this chapter have been changed by request to protect the participants' privacy.

Jennifer was surprised about having to spend so much time going over the definitions of character words. Since the children are exposed to a character development program at school, she thought that they would be more familiar with the words and their meanings. But Katherine, her seven-year-old, had to be helped with remembering what empathy, initiative, perseverance, and integrity meant. Anthony also had to be reminded that integrity was about remaining true to your beliefs.

Jennifer said that they "lost" both of their children "a bunch of times during the first session, which was too long." This feedback resulted in my shaping some of the sessions differently and reminded me to consider how important it is for parents to recognize what is a reasonable length of time for children to pay attention. This varies depending on the age and maturity of your child. Notice when their attention is waning and if necessary, take short breaks during the meeting or allow younger children to engage in a quiet activity as older children and parents continue to converse.

Unresolved Issues

Jennifer and her husband Alan, like many of the other parents who participated, found that family members often wanted to use these meetings as a forum to vent or express unresolved issues towards each other. For example, Anthony felt that he was taking on more than his fair share of responsibilities around the house, when compared to his younger sister, Katherine. On one of his worksheets, he wrote, "I show initiative by starting to dry the dishes without anyone asking but I think that Katherine should do more for the family." On another worksheet, he wrote, "I show fairness to the family by making things equal but I think that Katherine should do more."

As parents, it might be difficult not to jump in to defend a younger child or point out ways in which the critical child is not so perfect. However, if the integrity of a family meeting is to be maintained, if a parent is to model what he or she wants to see more of, then feedback needs to be carefully executed. I would suggest that if a similar scenario were to unfold in your house, that you acknowledge your disgruntled child's feelings with something like "It sounds as if you feel you are taking on more responsibility around the house than your sister and this doesn't feel fair." After his feelings are validated, you might say, "Over the next week, let's all think about what we can do as a family to help you feel that things are not so lopsided. At the next meeting we'll brainstorm about it." By responding in this way, you aren't having to immediately resolve your child's issue or take sides, but you are validating what he is feeling, showing that you want to find a solution, and modelling ways to resolve conflict.

Becoming More Aware

Once their involvement in the project was complete, I spoke to 10-year-old Anthony. He said that other than being able to vent his feelings towards his sister, he liked "expressing ideas and sharing them with the family. I actually learned something about myself. I learned that I can always be a good person. I realized that I treat people better than I thought I did. I wrote down an example about helping an old lady cross the street. I also learned that my mom, dad, and sister are mostly nice, even if they are sometimes pains."

Ultimately, Jennifer, Alan, Katherine, and Anthony gave The Family Plan a thumbs up. Jennifer said, "Thank goodness we had this wonderful opportunity to communicate. My children felt that, within the parameters of this exercise, it was okay to let us know about some things that are going on with them. Now we are empowered to do something about it."

Deena and Troy: Not Listening and Needing a Time-out

Not Listening

Deena and Troy are raising three teenaged children in a blended family. Two of the children, a son and daughter, are from Deena's first marriage and the third is Troy's son, one of his children from his first marriage. Deena said that their experience while participating in the exercises "was wonderful in many ways. We liked the group atmosphere and it was beneficial for all of us to sit and discuss our feelings and ideas." However, she admitted to sometimes finding their meetings "exasperating. I had to keep repeating myself. They weren't listening or one person was fiddling." Over the course of a few weeks, Deena started to realize that what she found most irritating in the meetings were similar annoyances to what she felt in everyday life—especially the not listening part.

At some point Deena concluded that *she* might be part of the problem and so decided that she was going to personally work on becoming more respectful by listening to, among other things, why specific chores hadn't been attended to. Deena realized that she didn't have the patience to listen to the same old excuses and often walked away from her family whenever they began by saying something that sounded familiar. She realized that she should instead say something like "I'm finding it frustrating to listen to this. I've heard it before. Can you tell me something else?"

Needing a Time-out

Deena's husband Troy came to realizations of his own. After feedback from his son and stepchildren, he concluded that he needed to work on being in a better mood when he arrived home from work. "I admit I'm not a barrel of laughs at the end of the day," he said. Troy was happy that the kids were able to share their feelings about his mood and was proud of himself for being able to listen to them without getting defensive. Their words helped him to become aware of an old pattern that he wanted to change. Troy and I discussed his need for a time-out after a long drive home. Ten minutes of alone time was all he said he needed to feel revitalized. I suggested that he purchase a red foam clown nose and wear it as he emerged from his bedroom after his time-out—an indication that he was in better humour and more approachable. I also offered him a round pin with a picture of one of the Seven Dwarves and "I'm Grumpy" written below the illustration, for him to wear when he didn't want to be approached.

The kids appreciated knowing what kind of mood they were going to find Troy in before they approached him and appreciated his sharing it in a humorous way.

Samantha and Max: Enhancing the Game Plan

Samantha and Max, a married couple with two boys aged 12 and 15, found that their involvement in The Family Plan deepened their ties as a family. Max said that they have always intentionally raised their children to possess the attributes of good character and Samantha believes that *modelling can even override innate temperament*. She said that when her 12-year-old son, Chuck, was a baby, he screamed and was colicky for seven solid months. "It was so bad that I didn't think I was even going to be able to go back to work. Later, they found that he fit the profile of a 'spirited child.'" They followed the strategies suggested in a book by the same name and actually shaped him with the techniques recommended by the author.

Today, Samantha and Max still implement strategies as a team and are consistent most of the time. Samantha says that part of how she has intentionally parented her children is with a lot of positive reinforcement. She'll say something like "Oh, that was so polite of you" or "Thanks for being back on time—that was so responsible."

Samantha said that taking part in The Family Plan made them more aware of the role that they have played in raising their sons to become the people they are today and also of how she and her husband are perceived by their children. "We try to be positive role models. Sometimes we say things that we regret, and then we apologize—no one is perfect, we realize that. But The Family Plan confirmed that we should keep doing the best we can. For example, if Max has had a difficult time at work and comes home to talk about standing up for what he believed in, I might say, 'It sounds like you acted with integrity.'" Samantha realizes that by using words like integrity in conversations with Max, her children learn how to use them too.

Overall, Samantha and Max felt that The Family Plan "solidified and enhanced what we've been doing all these years."

Shari and Tony: An Eye-opening Exercise

At first, Shari and Tony found it difficult to get their two teenaged sons, aged 16 and 14, to take the exercises seriously. At times she thought, "Oh my God, can we even get *through* these exercises? This is so painful and overwhelming!" Shari says that family meetings are foreign to them and that at the best of times, the boys feel uncomfortable about opening up about their feelings. However, once they got into it, they realized that it wasn't as touchy feely as they had feared and Shari and Tony found that behind their silly behaviour was "some good thinking. Daniel opened our eyes to some of what he was feeling by writing that 'What I have learned from watching others is that my family is often against me for showing a lack of empathy towards my brother, for example, but I realize that they have reason to be.'" He shared that even though he thinks that the attributes are important, they are often hard to live by.

Shari says that by the time the second meeting rolled around, things progressed far more smoothly than during the first and ended on a positive note. When Shari talked more about the importance of living lives of character and whether they believed it was worth the effort, she was relieved to hear that they both thought so. Daniel was very positive in believing that "everyone wants to do good."

After exploring and working on individual goals, Shari reported that for the most part, she felt that they were able to fulfill their individual goals. However, 16-year-old Daniel again said that living with good character felt too much like hard work and it was easier to be selfish. He felt that he "wasn't even close." Shari and Tony appreciated his honesty but felt that he was selling himself short. They were able to point out examples of times when he displayed good character naturally, without even working so hard. They reminded him of the many times that he had shown kindness towards his grandmother, for example. This, Shari said, seemed to encourage him in believing that being "good" wasn't so hard after all.

Shari said that her individual goal was to work on being more optimistic that her teens were going through a contentious stage they would soon outgrow. She thought she blew it when she confronted Daniel one day for not sharing with his brother, and he responded with a smirk. This fed into her anxiety about his future. She worried that Daniel as an adult might not be very nice to his partner. Then, because Dylan hadn't stood up to Daniel, she worried about Dylan's future and feared that he would let people walk all over him. I assured Shari that just because Daniel appeared not to be bothered when she chastised him for not sharing with his brother and just because Dylan didn't assert himself, that Daniel was not doomed to be uncaring and inconsiderate and Dylan was not doomed to live his life as a pushover. I assured her that their sibling rivalry was entirely normal. We also talked about the way in which she and Tony treat one another and how their respect towards one another—more than anything—would lay the foundation for how their sons treated their partners later in life.

Despite their sibling differences, Daniel shared that it is easier to talk to his brother than his parents. He finds him less judgmental and feels that they speak the same language. Daniel told his mom, "In your generation maybe I-messages work but in my generation they don't." Daniel feels that I-messages (a tool for communicating more effectively detailed in Chapter 9) are contrived. Dylan, on the other hand, believes that they *can* work and plans on using them.

The bottom line: though not every child bought into every technique, they all reported real benefits from The Family Plan, and all opened up more than they had before.

Lucia and Frank: It's Better with Both Parents on Board

When Lucia agreed to participate in The Family Plan, she was hoping that her husband, Frank, would be equally motivated. For years, she had been trying to impress upon him the importance of modelling respect and empathy—especially in front of their children. She saw this as an opportunity to get him on board. She was hoping that after participating in the exercises, Frank would understand that he could not continue with his "do as I say, not as I do" attitude. Lucia knows that if they are yelling, screaming, being sarcastic, and walking out of the room on one another, they are not teaching their children how to be respectful.

Tara, their eight-year-old, sees the way in which the family members relate to one another and wisely says, "We have to learn not to scream. When we get frustrated we take it out on each other. Mom told me when she screams in the future, to tell her and she will stop. I can see that she's working on that."

Frank did agree to take part but not as willingly as Lucia had hoped. In fact, he was away vacationing with a friend during one of the weeks they had agreed to participate. Lucia found it interesting to see the change in family dynamics when he was there versus when he was away. She realized that even she was more relaxed when he wasn't around. "I didn't have to work hard at cleaning up the mess after him."

Lucia saw a remarkable change in the children's behaviour as they worked through the exercises when Frank was away. When he came home, she noticed that the way in which the children related to each other and to adults in the family started to slip back to what it was before Frank left to go away. "We were so respectful of one another when he was away and now we are slipping back to our old ways." Along with showing disrespect, she shared that Frank shows a lack of responsibility. For example, first thing in the morning he might say, "Who took my shoes?" rather than "Has anyone seen my shoes?"

"He is blaming," Lucia said. "If I want to ask him something he'll snap and shout back, 'I'm busy. Can't you see? I can't do two things at once.' It draws me in, and then I snap at the kids because I'm angry at him."

Lucia recommended to Frank that they speak to a counsellor about their issues, which he agreed to. She has learned to respond to his behaviour differently and he has begun to see how his behaviour affects Lucia and their children.

Thus, even when The Family Plan doesn't go as smoothly as you might wish, it can reveal problems that need to be worked on, *and* point the way to solutions. After participating in this project Lucia was even more convinced that it is their modelling that matters most. She recognizes that their kids can be exposed to great material and modelling at school but when they come home, that wonderful feeling they had at school gets lost as they get drawn into unhealthy family dynamics. If the attributes are not being modelled at home, the children lose their benefit when they come through the door. Now that Frank has begun to face that realization too, things are improving for both parents and children.

Just like Lucia and Frank, Samantha and Max, Shari and Tony, Deena and Troy, Jennifer and Alan, and the other families that have already taken part in The Family Plan, you will find that along the path to learning and growing as a family of character, there will be many winding paths and sudden turns. Sometimes you will encounter inclement weather. Other times, you will bask in the warmth of your family's goodness. You may have to change direction or revisit an earlier destination before moving forward. There will likely be bumpy patches in between the smooth stretches, times to take a break and times to accelerate. Through it all, keep looking forward as your family takes this journey. It will create greater communication among you, advance your character goals, and allow you to feel closer to each other.

Short & Sweet

- Many of the older children who were asked to take part in The Family Plan were initially reluctant to engage in what they thought might be "touchy feely exercises." At the end, however, their feedback was very positive.
- When you're setting up your first family meeting, approach the process in a democratic way.
- Know that reluctance, especially at first, is normal. But it is often followed by enthusiasm for the open interaction and effective listening that takes place.
- When there are younger children in the family, it is especially important for parents to consider what might be a reasonable length of time for their children to pay attention.
- Family members will sometimes want to use these meetings as a forum to vent or express unresolved issues towards each

other; be prepared for this so that you can deal with it in a constructive way.

- Along the path to learning and growing as a family of character, there will be some rough patches. But even when The Family Plan doesn't go as smoothly as you might wish, it can reveal problems that need to be worked on, *and* point the way to solutions.
- All participants found that their involvement in The Family Plan advanced their goals as a family of character, and made them feel closer to each other.

Part Three

Chapter 11

Putting the Pieces Together: One Attribute at a Time

This section will provide a close-up of each of the ten crucial characteristics we've been looking at throughout this book. You have probably already begun to model many of them, but this section will provide a chance to focus on one at a time, and will also include fun activities for the whole family to engage in together so that they can experience and discuss each attribute.

Each chapter will begin with my thoughts, anecdotes, and experiences related to a particular attribute, and then offer some tips and suggestions about how you can further integrate that characteristic into your daily life. You may be surprised at how many opportunities there are to model the characteristic every day. As you move through the chapters, continue to add what you learn to your repertoire.

I suggest that you conduct your family meetings during the first week of every month. Prior to each meeting, encourage other adult members in the family to read the relevant chapter dealing with the specific characteristic. At the meeting, share the characteristic you would like to focus on with your children and ask for their co-operation. If they are unwilling, discuss why. If they feel that they are being forced into being there, acknowledge their feelings but encourage their participation by saying that the meeting will help them understand how to integrate the characteristic into their lives and share why it is so important.

You may begin, as with the weekly meetings, by bringing out your Family Plan binder. If you have been recording your meetings, you may want to continue doing so. You can rotate who chairs the meetings, but be aware that you may need to guide your children through the process sometimes, so that it remains democratic.

The conversational part of the meeting need only be 10 to 15 minutes long. Following this, engage as a group in the family activity for that month's characteristic. Encourage everyone to participate. The exercises, developed by Dynamix (a Canadian-based organization and the leader in team-building and character development for kids and teens), are explained in detail at the end of each chapter. They will allow family members to interact in the form of fun games and tasks that will put people in a non-defensive mood, ready to be open to each other's feelings and thoughts. The family activities offer great ideas to get you rolling, but you may want to invent others of your own—the possibilities are limitless.

At the end of each monthly meeting, complete a Monthly Meeting Worksheet (printed from www.characteristhekey.com). Following is an **example** of a Monthly Meeting Worksheet and how you might fill it out as a family:

MONTHLY MEETING WORKSHEET

DATE: ______________________________

CHARACTER TRAIT OF THE MONTH: **Perseverance**

WHAT WE LEARNED FROM THE DYNAMIX FAMILY ACTIVITY RELATED TO THE CHARACTER TRAIT OF THE MONTH IS THAT: **if we worked together, we were able to continue with the challenge for longer. It felt good to finally figure out how to reproduce the shapes. Dad was especially good at this.**

OUR PERSONAL GOALS FOR THIS MONTH AS RELATED TO THE CHARACTERISTIC OF THE MONTH:
Mom's goal: **To not give up on her ability to learn how to do Sudoku**
Dad's goal: **To not give up on Adam being able to learn how to skate**
Adam's goal: **To continue to skate even after he has fallen a million times!!**
Trish's goal: **To persist through her math homework even though she doesn't understand what algebra has to do with real life.**

In month two and going forward, I encourage you to look back in your Family Plan binder and discuss whether each person's personal goals were realized over the previous month and if not, why not. After this short discussion, move on to discussing the current month's characteristic.

In my household we have worked hard to build a vocabulary of character words and to use them whenever possible. When my daughter Chloe was nine years old, she helped me realize something important. She had begun working on her homework without being asked and I remarked, "Now that's showing initiative."

"Thanks for noticing, Mom," she responded, "but initiative was last month." Later, she said that she was only joking, but it made me think about how important it is to help our children understand that initiative, for example, doesn't need to be practised only during the month that a family (or a school) focuses on it; any and all of the attributes can and should be shown any day of the year. Ultimately, it's important to remember that the attributes, like pieces of a puzzle, work best when integrated into one, thus creating a whole person of character.

I have no doubt that as you see your family's beliefs and values grow in strength and clarity, as you notice behavioural changes that reflect their increased awareness of the value of good character, you will be further inspired to continue modelling with intention. That's part of what I meant in the Introduction when I said that the attributes of good character are "self-affirming." To model them with intention and to see your children display them makes you feel good about what you are doing.

And there's a further point. Children who live by these principles begin to experience and realize things differently so that they want to stay on course. Each attribute of character has a message within it, waiting to be decoded by the person who faithfully practises that maxim. A nugget of wisdom is there to be discovered, a piece of good news that makes life richer, more joyous, and more fulfilling. For example, acting with courage will bring you the surprising revelation that *the thing you feared only seemed so formidable because it managed to make you afraid.* The bully turns out to be a coward, but you can only discover that by facing him down. Once you've experienced what it feels like to act with courage, you never want to go back to a world without bravery. As I discuss each attribute, I will talk about the special dividend carried within it.

At this point in the process of learning to model character to your children, you are likely at the stage where you are aware of what you are doing, and aware that you are becoming more proficient at it. After a while the process will become "second nature" to you, literally a natural part of who you are as a person and as a parent. For now, it's enough that you are thinking more about how your actions affect your children and how they learn from them, and that you are continuing to adjust your own behaviour in order to teach what you want to see.

Keep going.

Chapter 12
Focus on Empathy

"Empathy is listening with our hearts to how someone else is feeling."
—Susan, mom to teen boys

Empathy is one of the most important attributes. We show empathy when we express interest in understanding another being's experience through their eyes, rather than our own. Although others' pain or pleasure in a sense belongs to them, we show empathy by asking questions and making an effort to imagine, validate, or acknowledge what they are experiencing without making it about ourselves. It is not necessary to have personally experienced the same situation or event in order to show empathy. When I asked children for their definition, they said things such as "Being able to put yourself in another person's shoes."

When a friend shares a particularly sad story and you wipe a tear away, you are showing empathy. You can imagine what the experience must have been like for him even if you have never experienced the same yourself. When you acknowledge your child's hunger pains even though you can't imagine how she could possibly be hungry so soon after dinner, you are modelling empathy.

Even if your immediate reaction to an experience your child is sharing is one of anger or concern, showing empathy requires that you put your judgments and comments aside for a while. For example, if your child talks about an incident at school that involved an angry exchange of words between herself and a friend, even if it is clear that your child has played a part in instigating the argument, this may not be the right time to discuss your concerns. All she is asking for is support and understanding. An empathetic response would be more like "You felt that she was really mean to you. Perhaps you felt embarrassed, especially in front of your friends. No wonder you were left feeling sad." This type of response will help your child feel as if you have put yourself in her position and will encourage her to talk about it some more or to at least feel acknowledged. As counsellors are taught, people are much more ready for problem-solving after their initial feelings have been listened to in a validating way. Whether adults or children, we need to know that someone hears what we are saying and sees how we could feel that way.

Helping the Less Fortunate

Living in the suburbs means that many children are less physically exposed to people who are not as fortunate. But when a winter drive takes them through meaner streets, kids will ask questions about the people who have taken up residence on pieces of cardboard on the snowy sidewalk. They will ask how they stay warm at night, what might have led up to them living on the street, and why their families are not taking care of them. It is good to answer their questions honestly, and try to develop their empathy for those who are less fortunate than themselves. What is even better is to model active participation in soup kitchens or food drives, for example, so that children can see that empathy is not passive, but active, that it isn't real unless it includes doing whatever you can to alleviate others' plight.

Caring and compassion can be modelled in any neighbourhood. Showing compassion by providing a meal, or being there to provide support and comfort to a neighbour who is sick or alone, are great expressions of empathy.

When my daughter was in elementary school, there was a specially designated class for children with autism. Children from the other classrooms, some as young as nine years old, were given the opportunity of spending time with these special needs children. A student named Francine told me about her experience. When she was 12 and in grade 7, she and some of her peers spent time with the autistic children, assisting the teachers during many of their recesses. "When I was younger," says Francine, "I was a little frightened of them because they made sudden noises and movements and I felt awkward being around them. Then once I started to know them and spent time with them, I didn't feel afraid or uncomfortable any more." Francine says that she learned a lot about being patient and about appreciating the small victories—like when one little boy mastered, with her help, being able to do up his zipper. She also learned "we are all different, and it takes some people a lot longer to do things that we take for granted." What a great way for kids to get to understand and empathize with others who are not as able-bodied or mentally capable as themselves.

In addition to having classrooms set aside, other schools often integrate special needs children into "regular" classroom settings. Having a child who is in a wheelchair share her experiences with other children who are more able-bodied has far greater influence in helping children develop empathy towards others than any lecture a teacher or parent could provide. Even having a child with diabetes or scoliosis give a mini-presentation on how her life is a little different or how and when she has to use insulin or wear a back brace is a great way of helping students see another's point of view.

Another good way for kids to exercise empathy is to take part in raising funds for charitable organizations. I believe, however, that when children raise funds, they should focus on the cause, the difficulty that will be alleviated, with the motive of helping others. I have a problem when charities or organizations offer prizes as incentives to those who collect the most amount of money in a fundraiser, with the more money collected, the greater the reward. I remember one day when my daughter brought home a charity's donation envelope from school, and the first thing she talked about was which of the prizes she wanted. She was more concerned about whether her collection would take her to the next level of prizes than she was about where the money was going and what it would do to help people in need. The (unfortunate) message to her was: help others and you will receive a material reward in exchange.

While this kind of competition can encourage children (and adults) to raise more money, the fundamental message about helping others without the need for a reward can often be lost. I would much rather help my child become more aware of the *intrinsic* rewards of helping others. For this reason, when fundraising requests like these come into our home, I make sure to remove the material prize incentive from the equation by donating what we can afford, making light of the material gift, and talking about how our money is going to help people in need.

Overcoming Violence

One need look no further than our living rooms and the video games our kids are playing to see what we are fighting against in our quest to develop empathy in them. Blood and guts spill from characters shot dead as our children engage in gory warfare against increasingly realistic enemies on the screen. You can read claims about the cathartic effect engaging in aggressive games has on children, but the flip side is that we run the risk of our children becoming immune to the effects of violence and the devastating impact that violent behaviour has on human beings in real life.

Pay close attention and you may be surprised at some of the brutal content in seemingly benign television programs that your children are watching, and at the disrespect and lack of empathy shown by some of the role models in their favourite shows. These characters are modelling too—just not the attributes we want.

Unfortunately, many kids are also exposed to acts of violence in real life—from bullying to domestic violence to racism to gangs. Lana Feinstein is the Executive Director at *Leave Out Violence* (LOVE), the leading not-for-profit youth violence prevention organization in Canada. They work with youths who have been victims of, perpetrators of, or witnesses to violence. Their website (www.leaveoutviolence.com) explains how the movement got started in 1993, "by a woman named Twinkle, whose husband was murdered by a 14-year-old boy. After dealing with her feelings of anger and sadness, she learned that the boy who killed her husband was also a victim of violence. In order to break the cycle of violence, Twinkle decided to spend her life helping youth learn to help themselves, and eventually how to help other youth as well." Now, that's taking empathy to great heights!

LOVE's goal is to help youths end the violence in their lives by understanding their own and others' behaviour and by providing them with alternatives to violence and teaching other ways of responding to strong emotions—anger, for example. Lana talks about a crucial step in helping some youths to develop their capacity for empathy. She says, "If you are engaging in violent behaviour, you are not thinking about the effects of your behaviour and long-term consequences. For example, a child who bullies may lack respect and understanding for the person they are bullying." The youths are helped through specialized programs in photojournalism, leadership training, and others, to learn new skills, become empowered to make positive change, and develop greater understanding of how violence affects others. They are given a voice so that they may become community leaders who can speak from personal experience and positively influence their peers—thus reducing violence in schools, neighbourhoods, and homes.

Another Lesson in Compassion

The earlier in our children's lives that we model—and encourage—behaviour that reflects empathy for all living things, the greater the chance that our children will become compassionate people. Sometimes, it takes just one incident to bring out a child's true colours. One mother, Luanne, told me a story of something that happened when her son was nine. Pete had not shown a lot of empathy for any living thing so far in his life. He tended to be mean to his sisters and poke a hole in their weak spots: his older sister thought herself too tall and he called her "the Bean Pole"; his younger sister was a pale redhead and he called her "Pasty." Luanne had tried to moderate his behaviours but without much luck so far. Then one Saturday morning a beagle dragged itself down the hill and into Luanne's driveway. She would have backed over it if Pete hadn't seen it.

He yelled, "Stop, Mom!" and ran behind the car. He came back carrying the dog in his arms. "I think his leg is broken," Pete said. "He was limping. He looks bad." The dog was dirty and thin, but it lay calm in the boy's arms, looking up at him with those big beagle eyes.

That day's plans were blown away as Luanne and her son cared for the dog. They made it a bed in a cardboard box and cleaned it up as best they could, then called a vet and arranged to take the dog in that afternoon. Luanne told me, "Pete kept looking at the dog and saying, 'He made it to our house, Mom. He knew he had to.'" Luanne saw something in Pete that she had never seen before—his superficial guard had come down and his compassion towards the dog shone through.

At the vet, the receptionist asked for the dog's name. Before Luanne could think, Pete said, "Braveheart." That was when Luanne started to sense that they were going to have a beagle in the family. But before they could adopt Braveheart, Luanne explained to Pete why it was the right thing to try to return him to his rightful owner first. So, they posted flyers and Pete prayed that no one would claim him.

For the next few weeks no one else could get near the dog when Pete was around. It turned out the leg had a bad sprain but it wasn't broken. The dog was undernourished, and it had to be given oral medicine for a touch of bronchitis. Luanne was surprised when Pete said he wanted to learn how to give Braveheart the medicine. Luanne said that was a great idea. He got very good at it, to the point where Braveheart would willingly open his mouth and Pete would pop the pill in, twice a day, like clockwork. Luanne and her husband watched all this with growing wonder.

No one claimed Braveheart, and he became their son's best friend. According to Luanne, Pete was never quite the same after that. When anyone was hurt—even his sisters—he would come to their aid. In fact, his sisters sometimes teased him about being a "softie" but Pete didn't seem to mind.

Pete's parents were thrilled that they had never given up hope, and that empathy for an injured animal had begun to open their son's eyes. They could tell that he was now on the road that leads to a moral outlook, where you can see that you should treat others in the way you would want to be treated, and that the world is not as good a place as it could be as long as someone is suffering.

The activity that follows will take about a half hour to complete. At the end of this activity, the whole family will have a better understanding of what it feels like to try to complete an activity while being challenged by a physical impairment. The goal is to help each family member experience what it feels like to be in the body of a person who is impaired in some way—in order to develop greater empathy.

Dynamix Family Activity
Enacting Empathy

Activity name:
Building Castles

Materials needed:
- Straws
- Masking tape
- Paper clips
- Construction paper
- Scissors
- Popsicle sticks
- Pens/pencils
- Cotton balls
- Other miscellaneous supplies or materials

Other options: A pile of pillows, building blocks, containers or any other items that can be stacked or placed on top of one another.

Set-up:
Place all the materials at one end of the room where the activity will take place. Throughout the activity, each

participant will simulate a different physical impairment. Consider the following options:

- Blindfolding a player so that he or she cannot see
- Placing oven mitts over the hands of a player so that he or she has difficulty using his or her hands
- Tying the hands of one player behind his or her back so that he or she cannot use them at all
- Asking one player to pretend not to be able to walk

One way to determine who takes on what challenge is to write the options on separate pieces of paper, and then have each person pull one out of a hat.

Directions:
In this activity, the family will be working towards building a castle with the items they have been given. When building this castle, each family member will simulate a different physical impairment. To add to the difficulty of this task, all of the items will be placed at the other end of the room. One at a time, a player will go over to the items, gather a few that will help build the castle and then return to the area where the castle is being built. Each player must continue to simulate his or her physical impairment throughout the activity. You might want to set a 20-minute time limit for this activity.

Discussion:
This is an incredibly powerful activity. It really opens people's eyes to the struggles that so many people in our

(*Continued*)

world face each and every day. Ask family members if they can imagine living with a real physical impairment such as the one he or she has adopted for the game and having to overcome their difficulties every day.

Some discussion questions:

- What sorts of impairments do you see people face in life?
- What "invisible" impairments do you know about? How do these affect people differently or the same as more visible impairments?
- Have you ever helped someone with an impairment? How?
- Are people with impairments any less likely to succeed in life?

Chapter 13

Focus on Fairness

"Live so that when your children think of fairness and integrity, they think of you."
—H. Jackson Brown, Jr.

One of the most common phrases heard from children is "It's not fair!": "It's not fair that he got extra French fries," "It's not fair that he gets to stay up later than me," "It's not fair that they get to see the movie and I don't."

Exasperated by this litany, parents may respond with comments such as "Get over it, life isn't always fair" or "What do you mean, not fair? Each of you has exactly the same number of French fries. I counted!"

Children place fairness high on their list of priorities. When children make these comments, they are saying that they feel that the scales of justice are not balanced. In fact, they are sometimes correct. If, for example, you expect them to make their beds but you don't make yours, you may want to adjust your behaviour to reflect what you want from them.

Practising fairness doesn't mean, however, that every time your child points out a discrepancy, you have to come up with an *explanation* of what you did. Sometimes all you need say is something like "It sounds as if you think I gave your brother more French fries and that makes you upset. Perhaps you'd like some more." Also, keep in mind that although you may try to model fairness most of the time, children may demand more than you can provide.

You may also want to consider whether trying to balance the scales all the time is realistic. For example, if you purchase a pair of shoes for your youngest because his have holes, how does his older sibling react? If you've established a precedent for always having to purchase the same or something of equal value for all of your children, you may be setting yourself up for trouble. Although fair means that you do not favour one child over the other, it doesn't mean you always have to buy the same thing for all of your children, *whether they are in need or not.* What is more relevant is that when it comes time to buy a pair of shoes for each, you shop at the same or similar stores and that you don't buy the most fashionable and expensive for one and the most outdated on the sales rack for another.

I am reminded of a story about a parent who, extremely proud of his son's success as a graduate of a medical program, rewarded him with a car as a gift. For a parent who has the financial means, this in itself is fine. However, when his younger son graduated from a culinary program several years later, his father presented him with a framed poster. The younger son felt that he had been discriminated against because of his choice of career. He realized that the gift of a car versus that of a framed poster spoke volumes about the way in which their father felt. Recognizing that our children may be better suited for one path over another and respecting their choices, even if they differ from ours or from what we had hoped for them, is an important part of modelling fairness.

When our children are fighting with one another, it is normal to want to jump in to protect a younger child or a child who seems less able to defend himself. However, this will also likely be perceived as "not fair" by the child who does not feel supported. Rather than taking sides, you may model fairness by remaining neutral and encouraging your children to work the issue out together or you may mediate by acknowledging how each is feeling and then helping them brainstorm solutions.

When it comes to disciplining, children have special radar for what is most fair or just. If you ground your child for a month because she lied to you, she will likely be quick to point out that you are not being fair, and perhaps she is right. This is why, as we saw in Chapter 3, logical and natural consequences work so well. Unlike rewards and punishments, which are arbitrary (and often unrelated) responses to behaviour that you approve or disapprove of, consequences require more thought and effort. They are directly related to the misbehaviour. They make sense. As a result, children are usually more inclined to accept the consequences and to comply with them. Punishments, on the contrary, often feel unfair, and as a result kids rebel against them.

I was at a dinner party not long ago, and the host commented on how much he hated being placed at the "kids'" table when he was a child. He felt that it wasn't fair, and that he was being treated as a second-class citizen. He didn't like being excluded from the "main" table and wished that there had been some way of integrating children and adults so that no one was left out or pushed aside. Although some kids may actually prefer to be in the company of their peers, rather than have to listen to boring adult conversation, I found his comment thought-provoking.

Children who are being raised in homes where fairness is modelled are often quick to point out inequality and discrimination around them. They may join clubs and take on causes that appeal to them. Unfortunately, as children, their hands are often tied. Their voices may not be as strong, may not be heard. This is where you can play a role in working with them and exposing them to organizations, clubs, and groups that empower children to express their concerns.

When children absorb the principle of fairness and begin to extend it, not just to themselves, but to others, they are on their way to an important insight: other people are just as important as ourselves.

The activity that follows will take about 20 minutes to complete. At the end of this activity, the adults and children will have a better understanding of what happens when items are not distributed fairly among all players and how each feels as a result.

Dynamix Family Activity
Enacting Fairness

Activity name:
Building Character Towers

Materials needed:
- Straws
- Masking tape
- Paper clips
- Construction paper
- Scissors
- Popsicle sticks
- Pencils/pens
- Cotton balls
- Other miscellaneous supplies or materials

Set-up:
Randomly distribute the materials to the players. Do not worry about being fair. In fact, make sure the result

is unfair! Perhaps one person will receive the majority of straws and some tape, while someone else gets stuck mostly with paper clips and cotton balls. Someone is sure to comment on how unfair you are being. Let him or her know that you are only doing what the exercise calls for.

Directions:
Tell the group that the goal of this activity is for each member of the family to build a tower that is taller than anyone else's.

Before building the towers, offer everyone in the family the opportunity to trade materials with each other. Let them know that this is not essential and that no one should be forced into trading with another. Set a time limit for the trading process—approximately three minutes. Once the trading is done, it's time to build the towers! The tallest tower wins!

Discussion:
What's crucial in this activity is the discussion *after* the tower building is complete. Ask the children if they think this challenge was fair. Why or why not? What does fair really mean? Were they not given the same opportunity to win? Were they not able to trade for materials they thought would help? So then, ask: what is *not* fair? What would have been a more fair way to conduct this activity? Should everyone have received the same materials?

Chapter 14

Focus on Courage

"With courage you will dare to take risks, have the strength to be compassionate and the wisdom to be humble. Courage is the foundation of integrity."

—Keshavan Nair

Courage doesn't mean not being afraid. It means moving ahead even though you *are* afraid, and that often involves acknowledging and facing your fear, so that you can overcome it. That in turn isn't easy, because feeling scared is one of the most unpleasant experiences humans know, so we'll do almost anything to avoid it. A sort of reflex makes us hide from our fears and think of excuses for not doing something we are afraid of.

Not all fear is bad. Nature equips us with lots of fears that help us survive—what we might call *rational fears*. For example, campers who are afraid of bears and therefore don't keep food in their tent are less likely to attract bears. This is rational. What we need to overcome are the *irrational* fears—the ones that stop us from doing things we truly want or need to do, or should do. Or things we would really enjoy and benefit from, if we could just get started on them. Lastly, we need to try to overcome *phobias*—fears of specific things that trouble us out of all proportion to the potential harm.

Several types of circumstance can easily trigger fear—for example, when we've done something before and had a negative experience. A small boy gets jumped on or bitten by a dog, and is afraid of all dogs for years, thus losing out on all the fun canines offer. A young girl paints a picture and it gets laughed at by an older sibling, so she becomes wary of expressing her creativity in the future. By noticing and understanding these kinds of events, parents can help children understand their negative trigger and learn to work through their fear.

A second circumstance that often triggers fear is when we face the unknown. Life throws a lot of challenges at us that take us into unfamiliar territory, and it's natural to be afraid of what may be lurking there.

Interestingly, we often fear that which we want most of all. Going after our deepest dreams can be terrifying—until we do it. And that is when courage is especially important. An acclaimed professor told me the story of how he got started as a teacher when he was a graduate student. He was given an instructorship to teach a class of 30 undergraduates three times a week. He was so scared the day of his first class that he stood out in the hall, looking in at the students, unable to breathe properly. Summoning his bravery, he forced himself to enter and began to talk. He noticed that his legs were shaking beneath him. To hide this, he retreated behind the desk and continued to speak. He also noticed, however, that his voice was *not* shaking. He slowly became more comfortable. His mind, thankfully, was clear. He said something witty and got his first laugh, and the next class wasn't as hard. This man turned out to be a born teacher, loved by his students, and was able to make difficult things clear to anyone who wanted to understand. He realized eventually that he had been so afraid of teaching because he *wanted* it so much and was afraid of failing.

As I mentioned in Chapter 11, when you summon bravery and face the situation, you often discover that what you feared wasn't as awful as you thought: it only seemed that way *because it made you afraid.* When faced down, the bully turns out to be a coward; the scary challenge can even turn out to be your heart's desire.

What you're willing to stand against is important; what you are ready to fight *for* also matters. A coward isn't someone who is afraid, or even who backs down sometimes; a coward is someone who won't defend what he or she believes in, or what he or she holds precious. So courage and integrity go hand in hand.

Parents who are seen facing scary things in their own lives—the challenge that threw them before, the unknown, the daunting dream, or the hostile opponent—and not caving in, are modelling the right stuff.

If your children see you avoiding challenges, and maybe not even admitting you're afraid, they will follow your example. Much better that they should learn that parents have fears too, and can summon the courage to face them. If you receive notification that you've been laid off from your job, for example, your first reaction may be terror—what if you're unable to find something else? What if the family income is no longer enough? You may feel a blow to your self-esteem, a sense that no employer out there is going to want you. So the fear of humiliation may take hold too. But you still have a choice as to how you present this news to your family, and what you end up modelling. After you've had a chance to recover your equilibrium, you may elect to say something like "Of course it's scary going on the job market, and it's not going to be easy, but I know that I can handle it, and I'm going to give it all I've got." Thus you model courage and optimism.

Boys in particular are taught to hide all fear, never to admit it because that's supposedly "being a sissy." So it's valuable if a father can be comfortable admitting that something scares him, and yet can go on to try it anyway. F.D.R. famously said, "The only thing we have to fear is fear itself." Because admitting one's fears is itself so scary, it's extremely valuable for a family to be able to discuss fears openly and know that no one is going to be mocked or humiliated. It's a good step on the road to courage, and it confers on us another of life's lessons: that fears, when you acknowledge and confront them, become smaller.

The activity that follows will take about a half hour to complete. At the end of the activity, family members will have gained greater insight into their own fears and those of others, and will have considered how important it is to face one's fears in order to overcome them.

Dynamix Family Activity
Enacting Courage

Activity name:
Fear Field

Materials needed:
- Three small pieces of paper per family member
- Blindfolds for each family member (bandana, cloth, etc.)
- Marker
- Bristol board
- Scissors
- Glue

Set-up:
Have all family members sit separately to write a different fear on each of their three pieces of paper. The fears can be anything they fear in life, at school, at work, at home, etc.

They can be simple and specific, such as a fear of spiders or thunderstorms, or more complex such as not wanting to attend social gatherings. Once all the fears have been written down, crumple each one up into a little ball. Find a space in the house where you can conduct this activity (approx. 10 ft x 10 ft) and then randomly spread the "fear balls" all over the designated playing area.

Directions:
The goal of the activity is for each member of the family to make their way through all the "fears" to the other side. However, when walking through the fears, they will be blindfolded. Every time they step on a "fear," family members will take turns picking up that fear ball. After all of the fear balls have been collected from the floor, come together as a group and have each person open up the balls that he or she has collected and read them out loud. Take a guess at which family member wrote the fear down. Make sure not to tease or put anyone down for feeling the fear. Instead, compliment the member on having the courage to share the fear. Then take part in the following discussion:

Discussion:
- Just talking openly about fears is courageous.
- When did the family member first experience the fear?
- What are different ways to begin to face the fear?
- Are we born with courage or can we learn it?

Chapter 15

Focus on Honesty

"Honesty is the first chapter in the book of wisdom."
—Thomas Jefferson

One of the chapters in my first book, *Am I a Normal Parent?*[1], is entitled "I'll Be There In a Minute . . . and Other Lies We Tell Our Kids." You have no idea how conscious I have become every time I tell my children, "I'll be there in a minute" and of how conscious my children have become too! They'll say things like "And we're supposed to believe that?" or "How many minutes will you *really* take to finish what you're doing?" Of course, we don't mean to lie when we say we'll be there in a minute. It's really just a figure of speech, used to buy extra time. Buying time is just one of the many reasons that parents are not always honest with their children.

Parents also lie to protect, such as when we buy an identical replacement goldfish before our child has noticed the dead one lying at the bottom of the tank. We don't always tell the truth because we are afraid of the consequences. We may want to avoid a tantrum so we say that we're out of chocolate chip cookies, rather than saying, "No, you'll have to wait until after supper," or we prolong stories about tooth fairies long after our children are ready to hear the truth.

Although we don't think twice about many of the lies already mentioned, the consequence of our children uncovering the truth is that trust is diminished. When your daughter discovers a packet of chocolate chip cookies at the back of the cupboard, she may storm off and dramatically swear that she'll never trust you again!

There are other more premeditated forms of dishonesty. For example, when you ask your child to slide down in the back seat of your car as you drive through the gates of the amusement park so that you can say that he's younger than he really is, consider the lesson that your child is receiving on honesty.

Lies, however, can't be avoided completely. People who are *totally* honest have trouble functioning in society and can even be classified as pathological, or at best "brutally" honest (consider the lead character in the TV series *House*). Normal adults (unlike young children) sometimes shade the truth to avoid hurting or offending someone or to avoid revealing too much about themselves. Perhaps a kind way of putting this is to say that we "edit" what we say. However, honesty should be the default: most of the time it is mandatory, especially in situations where someone else is relying on what you say, or where serious consequences depend on it. Our favourite friends are often the ones we can be most honest with.

Even when untruths slip through, they can often be turned into opportunities to teach something positive. For example, if on some occasion you lie in front of your kids to get out of accepting an invitation to someone's home, you can create a valuable lesson. If you were motivated by kindness not to tell the truth, you may want to tell your children that you lied so that you would not hurt the person's feelings. At the same time, however, you can admit to not being proud of your lie. Invite your children to help you think of better ways to handle such situations. For example, instead of making up a falsehood, "I can't come over because I have to be out of town that weekend," find a way to be kind but truthful. A good solution would be something like "I regret that I won't be able to make it." It's okay, and even beneficial, for kids to see that we view ourselves as a work in progress. Nobody's character is perfect. Striving to be a better person is a lifelong process.

Making children say things they don't really mean does not instil honesty. I often hear parents forcing their children to say "sorry": "Say sorry to your friend—hitting hurts"; "Say sorry to your sister. You can't push her like that"; "Say sorry to the dog for pulling his tail."

Most children comply because they feel they have no other choice. "Sorry," they'll say, with no emotion. "Say it like you mean it!" the parent often demands. "I said *sorry*," the child manages with a greater show of emotion. "Okay, now go play," says the parent and the child runs off, having capitulated. In this kind of situation, however, I wonder if parents are actually teaching their children to be *dishonest*. "Sorry" should be the result of a heartfelt emotion. Apologizing just because you are being forced to do so means that you learn how to kiss and make up and then move on, but it certainly doesn't mean that you're truly sorry. In fact, I'd prefer that parents say something like "Do you feel bad or sorry for what you did?" and then be open to the child's answer, even if it is no. Perhaps it is better to respect them for their honesty than force them to be phony.

Honesty can be a lonely road when one's peers aren't on it. I am reminded of the time when my then 17-year-old daughter came home after a test at school and shared how she had observed many of her classmates cheating. The teacher, she said, either had not seen what they were doing or was turning a blind eye, to avoid having to confront them. My daughter was struck by how she might easily score a lesser grade than those who had cheated. My guess was that she was torn between doing the "right" thing, even if that meant not getting as high a grade, versus the "wrong" thing in order to achieve the same "successful" results as her cheating peers.

Thomas Lickona writes about Hal Urban, a teacher at Woodside High School in Redwood City, California, who would likely relate to Talia's concerns. According to Lickona, Urban hopes to inspire his students to understand why honesty really is the best policy. Recognizing the difficulty in getting teenagers to buy into this when they see others seemingly getting ahead by lying or cheating, Urban encourages them to think about their behaviour by asking specific questions such as:

- Is "everybody's doing it" a valid reason to be dishonest?
- What are some of the rewards of being honest?
- What are some of the consequences of being dishonest?

Students are asked to discuss their answers in small groups and then as a class. Urban then hands out an essay he has written entitled "Honesty Is Still the Best Policy," which talks about the costs of dishonesty, such as how it can ruin a relationship, and the rewards of honesty, such as enabling us to be authentic. After reading the essay, the students, once again, record their answers to the original questions and discuss the reasons why they might have changed their minds after reading the essay.[2]

When Talia and I used the same questions for discussion, she realized that regardless of her score, she would be able to take full credit for it by not cheating. She realized that the grade would be a true reflection of how much she knew and that ultimately, this, along with being a person of character, was better than being a fraud.

Talia was right because in the final analysis, truth is more important than personal advantage. We humans have been given a precious gift—the gift of being able to communicate with each other—and when we lie, we sully that gift, and we disrespect ourselves and the person we deceive. When we tell the truth even though it puts our interests at a disadvantage, we honour what it means to be human.

You may be freer to be honest with your child than you think. A parent who took part in The Family Plan shared this story. One day her son told her that he thought she should try to be more honest. She was taken aback since honesty is something she has always prided herself on. When she asked him why he felt this way, he said, "Because I don't think that you tell it like it is." When she asked for an example, he told her that when he had recently asked her for feedback on an original song he had sung and played on his guitar, he remembered her saying that what she liked best was the "beautiful tone of his voice" but that some part of it wasn't "entirely clear." He said he felt that she was not being honest. He didn't want her to mince words but wanted to hear the "real truth" even if it wasn't as pleasant.

After some probing and finding out what she really meant, he asked, "Why didn't you just tell me that the lyrics didn't make sense? When you begin with something nice, I feel that you are just trying to soften the blow and you are just trying to protect me from the truth." She was surprised that he interpreted this as being dishonest but told him that she would take what he said into consideration. The following couple of weeks were a challenge as she held herself in check and changed direction each time she thought of buffering the not-so-nice truth with something pleasant.

Nowadays, any time she slips back into her old pattern, he asks, "What are you *really* trying to say?" Their discussions have helped her realize that after all the years of building his self-esteem, he has thicker skin than she gave him credit for. She realizes that he does not want her to buffer the truth with niceties—that he, in fact, associates this with being dishonest.

I remember a time when I was maybe 11 or 12 years old and sitting with my father in the car. We had just returned home and he was sharing something with me that he knew my mother wouldn't be happy about. I can't remember what—it may have been as benign as having bought something that he knew she would feel was too extravagant. Despite not remembering the secret, I vividly recall how I felt after he told me, "Don't tell your mom. I know she'll be angry." In fact, it was I who was left feeling most angry. I was angry at him for taking me into his confidence and then asking me to keep his secret, to take his side against my mother. I felt caught in the middle. Although I didn't want to go against him, to betray his confidence or disappoint him by not being able to keep his secret, I also did not feel that it was fair that I should be asked to keep something from my mother. If I had known then what I know now, I would have told him how I felt about being asked to be dishonest. As an adult looking back on this childhood memory, I believe that my father might have been surprised by my reaction. Although loving and supportive, my parents were not the most intentional in their approach to raising us. In fact, they were not unlike many parents raising their children 40 or more years ago. Today, things are different.

At an appearance on CBC's *Steven and Chris* show, I chatted with the hosts about how parents should handle kids' awkward questions and situations. The bottom line, I said, whether responding to "Mom, will you die?" or "Mom, will you and Dad get divorced one day?" or "How are babies made?" or "Do you think I'm fat?" is to be honest. Give your children the answers that they are requesting in a truthful but age-appropriate manner, using words and language that they can understand and relate to. For example, if a child is asking about how babies are made, don't say that you'll tell him when he's older. If he doesn't get the answer from you, he'll get it from his friends (and it may not be correct).

Suppose your child asks you whether you are going to die. Hard as it is to tell the truth, you might want to say something like "All living things die but I am not going to die for a long, long, long, long time." That is usually reassuring enough for children to hear. If your child asks if you think she is "fat" and you tell her that she is "just perfect," she will likely respond with "You have to say that, you're my parent!" Instead you might say something like "I don't like the word fat. Are others calling you that or is that what you think?" You might also say, "Some people weigh more than others. What matters more is if you feel that you are an attractive and healthy weight for yourself. Does your weight bother you?" And if your child says yes, you might ask, "What can we do to help you feel better?"

As the guitarist's mother in this chapter found out, children feel more secure with our feedback and answers when they can count on us to be honest with them.

The activity that follows will take about a half hour to complete. In the discussion portion, your family will have the opportunity to explore how much you trust one another to tell the truth—especially when given the opportunity to lie. You will also explore the impact of being honest or dishonest when working towards a personal versus a collective goal.

Dynamix Family Activity

Enacting Honesty

Activity name:
Let's make a trade!

Materials needed:

- Five cards (for each player), namely an Ace, Two, Three, Four, and Five, from a deck of playing cards. (If you have more than four participants, you will need more than one deck of cards.)
- A stopwatch or timer

Set-up:
Combine all of the playing cards (the specified five cards per player times the number of players). Shuffle the cards and then deal them—one at a time in a clockwise rotation—to each player. Once all the cards have been dealt, each player should have five cards. Some may be duplicates of others.

Have a timer or stopwatch ready to time Rounds One and Two of this challenge. Once you have read and understood the instructions below, be sure to set the timer or stopwatch so that you can time how long it takes before someone wins Round One and then the group completes Round Two.

Directions:
Before you begin this activity, ask everyone to check their sequence of cards to make sure that no one has coincidentally received cards Ace through Five. Although the players do not need to necessarily show their hands,

ask everyone to be honest and to admit if they have this sequence. If they do, re-shuffle and reassign the cards.

Before beginning play, start the timer or stopwatch.

The goal in Round One of this challenge is for each player to collect five cards: Ace, One, Two, Three, Four, and Five. The suits and colours of the cards are not relevant. This is accomplished by trading cards with other players. A trade takes place in the following manner.

Starting with the dealer and then moving clockwise, each player, one at a time, requests a trade from another player. So for example, the dealer may ask the player across from him/her, "Can you give me a Three?" (In fact, the dealer may be bluffing to throw his or her opponents off and may not even need a Three.) The player who is asked for a Three does not have to give the dealer a Three even if he has one. (He could have a Three but may also bluff that he doesn't.) He does, however, have to give up one of his cards. (We'll assume he gives the dealer something other than a Three.) At this point, the dealer will have six cards in his hand, the other player four. Then the roles reverse and the player who was originally approached asks the dealer for a certain numbered card and now the dealer has the choice as to whether he/she is going to help the other player or not.

When making the decision as to whether or not he wants to help the other player (if he has the card being requested), the dealer will have to consider whether or not he believes that the other player really did not have the Three he requested or if he chose not to help him. If he believes the latter to be true, he may choose to reciprocate

(*Continued*)

in spite—by not giving the player the card that is being requested, even if he has it.

Once the trade is made (i.e., each player has requested a card and given a card to the other player), each will be back to holding five cards.

Now, the next player in the circle (moving clockwise from the dealer) repeats the process by picking someone else in the circle to trade with. The game continues until one player has collected the correct sequence, Ace through Five. Once a player has all of the five cards required to win the round, he/she should place the cards face up in front of him/her. Stop the timer or watch to see how long you have been playing.

Then collect all the cards and have the dealer redistribute them as he/she did in Round One. In Round Two, the goal of the activity changes. This time, the desired goal is to see how many people in the group can collect a series of playing cards numbered Ace through Five in a five-minute period. It is very important to emphasize that in this round, the only win is if the entire group can work together at completing this challenge within five minutes. Once a player has all of the five cards, he/she should place the cards in front of him/her. Keep going to see how many other players will be successful in the time period allocated. Stop the timer at five minutes (or sooner if the goal has been reached) to determine how successful the group was at working together.

The main idea in this challenge, and where honesty comes into play, is that in Round One, each individual's goal is selfish, which may motivate him/her to be dishonest.

In Round Two, the goal is to work together as a group towards a collective goal. It is no longer in anyone's "best interest" to be deceitful or dishonest. So, if you need a Three, you will ask for a Three, because you know that is what you will get—since you are all in the game together and will play honestly. The contrasting rounds help to demonstrate how much more difficult the same task can be when we are not honest or helpful.

Discussion:

- How successful was the trading between each of the players during the first round?
- How many winners were there in the first round?
- Was the first round more challenging than the second? Why?
- Did you comply with your family members' requests in the first round? Why or why not?
- How did your approach change in Round Two?
- Were more people playing honestly in Round Two? Why?
- How long did it take for the first player to reach his/her goal in Round One, when the members didn't always make an honest trade?
- Did the group manage to reach their goal in five minutes or less in Round Two? Why do you think that worked so well?
- When you know that others have the option to lie or tell the truth, do you give them the benefit of the doubt by thinking that they will be honest and helpful, or do you think that they will lie to help themselves? Why?

Chapter 16

Focus on Initiative

"If your ship doesn't come in, swim out to meet it."
—Jonathan Winters

Taking initiative occurs as a result of two primary influences. The first and most important is learned. If children observe their parents making the first move towards getting the job done, helping others, and making dreams become reality, then they are more likely to do the same. It's good for children to see parents extending themselves beyond their home and into the community; to see them making first moves in creating change, in taking action, in helping to carve out their destiny. Examples would be helping to establish and then attending meetings to fight a problem in one's community, or something as simple as introducing oneself to new neighbours.

The other factor is self-confidence, which is closely linked to a person's self-esteem. As usual, modelling and encouragement are huge factors. If children see their parents acting with confidence, they will be more likely to behave in the same manner. If a child is encouraged ("Thanks for taking your dish and cutlery and putting them in the dishwasher without being asked") when she acts in a way that is consistent with taking initiative, she is likely to do so more often. If a child is helped to feel good about him or herself ("Trust yourself. You usually make mature, informed decisions"), she is more likely to have the confidence to take initiative.

Since taking initiative means that you are the first to make a move, there are often risks associated with it. If your children see you taking risks and dealing well with the consequences of things not always going according to plan, they will be more inclined to take risks too. The more secure one feels about paving the way, taking first steps, and making sound decisions, the more likely one is to take initiative. When either of my daughters makes comments such as "But no one else is doing that," I often respond with "Are you a leader or a follower?" I don't mean to suggest that everyone should be a leader all the time. Sometimes allowing others to lead is appropriate too, depending on their level of expertise and knowledge. However, I want my children to have the capacity to act independently and not to allow others to negatively influence their dreams and ideas.

In a way, procrastination is the opposite of initiative. When we procrastinate, we see an obvious task that needs doing, or a need that wants filling, but we think of a host of reasons for putting it off: it isn't the right day for it; it's a challenging job and we may not do it perfectly; it's going to take too much energy and we're tired; there's a more fun (and easier) thing to do right now. But these are dangerous stances to model for our children. They point to a world where work piles up undone, and challenges get ducked. Better that our kids should see us dive happily into rewarding activity and welcome the productive use of energy.

Energy. Sometimes it seems in short supply, but maybe that's the surprise that initiative carries within it: the good news that the more we leap into positive action, the more energy we will have. People often say that if you want something done, give it to a busy person. Energy begets energy.

The activity that follows will take 20 to 30 minutes to complete. The goal of this exercise is to determine if your children take initiative, without prompting, when they know there is a need to prepare for an activity. You will have an opportunity to discuss this with them prior to and following the activity.

Dynamix Family Activity

Enacting Initiative

Activity name:

Picture Perfect?

Materials needed:

- Scissors
- Markers
- Printable activity sheets, answer sheet, and instruction sheet (available at www.getdynamix.com/characteristhekey)

Set-up:

About a week before your meeting, print the sheets needed for this activity. Use a magnet or tape to display

(*Continued*)

the printed activity sheets on your fridge, or some place else for everyone in the family to see. Be sure to only hang the worksheets and instruction sheet and NOT the answer sheets. Put those aside for when you actually conduct the activity.

Directions:

A few days before this month's family meeting, casually mention to your family members that the family activity is going to require some preparation. Make sure that they know where to find the sheets (including instructions) related to the activity and that they know where to locate the other materials such as scissors and markers. *Do not specifically ask them to help out.*

The instruction sheet will explain exactly what to colour and what to cut out in preparation for the activity.

Do not remind your children about needing to prepare for this task again. The idea is to see if they will take the initiative to prepare on their own, without being prompted again. Just prior to the family meeting, before setting up the activity, check to see if your children took initiative to prepare the materials. There are two possible outcomes:

1. They prepared the materials. If this happened, congratulate them for doing an outstanding job of taking initiative, get right into the activity and enjoy!
2. They didn't prepare the materials. In this case, it is important to have a talk about initiative. Tell them that because no one took initiative to prepare the

materials in advance, the activity you have planned for them will need to be delayed for a short time. Now go ahead and ask the children to help.

When the materials are ready, begin the activity. Initiative has already been dealt with prior to the beginning of this exercise. The exercise itself is not specifically related to taking initiative.

Picture Perfect?

Rules:

- Have pairs of players sit back to back. Player A in each pair has an answer sheet, while player B has the corresponding cut-out pieces. (If there is an odd number of players, either take turns, or have two players sitting side by side and the third player back to back with the pair. The pair will share the responsibility on their side. Another possible solution is for a parent to sit this one out and be the "judge," ensuring that all the rules are being followed.)
- Without the partners turning to face each other, or showing each other their sheets or materials, the player with the answer sheet must try to describe to the other player how to arrange his or her cut-out pieces to match the picture on the sheet.
- The player with the cut-out pieces is not permitted to speak at all.
- Once the player with the cut-out pieces feels that he or she is done, he or she can turn to see the answer sheet.
- Play a few rounds with different answer sheets, so that everyone gets a chance to try both roles.

(*Continued*)

NOTE: At the end of the game, watch to see if anyone takes initiative to clean up!

Discussion:

- At which point in this exercise would taking initiative have been helpful? And how would taking initiative have helped everyone?
- What other opportunities can you think of where taking initiative would make the situation better?
- How do people feel when others take initiative?
- Why do some people take initiative and others don't?

Chapter 17

Focus on Integrity

"I believe that respect and integrity are among the most important of the traits. Respect because it teaches you how to interact with others and integrity because it teaches you how to interact with yourself."
—Arthur Birenbaum, teacher

Integrity means having a solid centre that others can count on, that remains consistent in the face of contrary forces—a set of values, beliefs, and purposes that, like a stone fortress, can't be shaken by life's winds and storms. A person of integrity may occasionally be seen as annoying or difficult, because they won't bend to the will of the moment, but in the end they are a rock on which others can rely, a source of strength to lean on, and an example of wholeness to be inspired by.

The ability to form a plan and then stick to it is part of integrity. So many times in life, in little and big ways, we are knocked off (or almost knocked off) the track we've chosen. A mother is intending to go straight home after work, but a co-worker says, "We're heading for the pub, join us." A dad is starting a new diet, but on the third day the kids want pizza, and it smells so good. Life is chock full of these potential derailments, these tests of resolve. Our reactions to them are the everyday benchmarks of integrity.

One of the most powerfully challenging forces to integrity is the youth peer group. It is very hard for a teenager, in particular, to stand against whatever their peers think is cool. One high school student said to me that an example of showing integrity occurs "when a friend says, 'Let's smoke,' and you stand up for your beliefs and say 'No, smoking is bad and I'm not going to do it'—even if it means giving up your friendship." She is so right, and we parents can help our children get to that level of self-trust. When our children see us "sticking to our guns" and not being lured away from our own worthwhile plans and purposes, they learn what integrity means, and what it costs.

Speaking of costs, principles mean the most when they are *inconvenient*. I remember when my husband and I started dating, over 25 years ago, and he was a chiropractic student working part-time in the men's shoe department of The Bay in downtown Toronto. As a young girl in love, I could sit for hours watching him interact with his customers. Although I couldn't put it into words back then, I now know that it was partly his work principles and beliefs that attracted me. There can be a lot of pressure in sales positions to hustle the customers to the cash register by telling them what they want to hear. In spite of all that, he preferred to spend extra time with each customer, making sure that their shoes fit perfectly and providing exceptional service. Even now, many years later, he treats his chiropractic patients in the same way. Making sure that he takes time with each patient and ensuring that they are being helped is what makes him happy. And that doesn't surprise me, because he demonstrated his loyalty to his own values back then, when it wasn't the easiest or even the safest way.

If integrity is a kind of "loyalty to oneself," it can also involve loyalty to others. Do we abandon our friends when that is the political thing to do? Or do we stand with them even when it means others may turn away from us? Many a kid in the playground has had to face this choice, when his or her BFF suddenly falls out of favour with the popular kids. Humiliation is a powerful sword, and it takes a brave soul to face it for someone else.

A *brave* soul. That illustrates the way integrity can often embrace the other character traits that we have looked at. The question becomes: do we hold fast to courage, honesty, fairness, and respect, even when it's difficult, when we could cut corners and have an easier time? When we answer a resounding yes and stand up for a person or a principle, we receive the special bonus that integrity gives: an unshakable confirmation of which things are truly precious.

Part of integrity is having consistent principles across the board, and not just selecting *some* of them. Berkowitz and Bier write, "No school would feel successful if its graduates were altruistic and caring but cheated routinely, nor if they were scrupulously honest but sadistic bullies. This notion of *coherence* in character is what many mean when they speak of a person's integrity."[1]

Acting with integrity means you aren't just trying to impress others. When Dr. Mike Thomson,* founder of *It's All About Character* talks to groups of children about character, he says, "The classic definition of good character is when you make good choices even when no one is watching." He tells them, "It's easier to make good choices in front of mom and dad, but the true test of your character is when you show integrity, or make good choices, when you're not being watched."

Of course, the same is true for parents.

* Dr. Mike Thomson is a nationally acclaimed speaker, author, and founder of www.itsallaboutcharacter.com. He works with schools, businesses, and communities that want to develop good character and ethics by teaching, enforcing, advocating and modelling principles to others in order to make a difference.

One mother told me that if she wants her children to stand up for their values, she needs to work on her own integrity, even when her kids aren't around. "I am willing to be a chameleon to get what I want, or even to make *other people* happy. Sometimes that's the fault with us parents—we want to please everybody!"

If, in spite of all the forces that impinge, you choose to be a parent who acts with integrity, your children will see you as a solid support. They will respect and admire you for your convictions and even though they may not always like what you stand for, they will appreciate knowing that they can rely on you to consistently live within a specific framework of beliefs. In a deep sense, they will know *who you are.*

The activity that follows will take approximately 20 minutes. At the end of the activity, your family will have the opportunity to discuss the importance of being true to oneself and each other and to discuss the consequences of not maintaining one's integrity.

Dynamix Family Activity

Enacting Integrity

Activity name:

Rope shapes

Materials needed:

- One five to 10-foot rope

Set-up:

Tie the ends of the rope to each other to create one large circle.

Directions:

To start the activity, everyone must stand in a circle, close their eyes, and hold on to the rope (in front of them). Taking turns and with eyes closed, each person calls out a shape and then everyone tries to create that shape with the rope. For example, if family member A calls out "SQUARE," the family must try to get the rope into the shape of a square. This can be done by stretching your arms out further, or closer; perhaps by moving backwards, or forwards, until everyone thinks that the rope is in the shape of a square. When your family is done, continue to keep your eyes closed and carefully place the rope, in the requested shape, on the floor. After you have all let go of the rope, open your eyes and check out your masterpiece. REMEMBER, the key to this activity is keeping your eyes closed. Even when you know you can get away with peeking, do you? Only you are responsible for maintaining integrity throughout the activity.

Discussion:

- Was this activity easy or hard? Why?
- Did you find it hard to keep your eyes closed the whole time? Why?
- Was there a time that you wanted to peek really badly? Explain.
- Why did/didn't you peek?
- Why is it important to follow the rules of a game?
- Why is it important to be honest with yourself (i.e., show integrity)?

Chapter 18

Focus on Optimism

"A pessimist sees the difficulty in every opportunity. An optimist sees the opportunity in every difficulty."
—Sir Winston Churchill

Optimism is tricky. Like courage, it's a great attribute, but it needs not to fly in the face of the facts. Denying global warming may be optimistic, but it won't stop it from happening. Facing possible bad outcomes and admitting that they are real is often the only way to prevent them. If the weather forecast says it's going to rain tomorrow, it's a good idea to put up a tent for the wedding reception: then even the optimists will be dry. Those who think financial bubbles will never burst and real estate prices will always keep rising sometimes end up losing their homes. Optimism untethered to reason is the definition of why casinos make so much money.

So what am I recommending when I extol the virtue of optimism? I mean two things:

1. When a good outcome is perfectly possible or even usual, believing in it makes it even more likely; and

2. Even when a good outcome is far from guaranteed, if you know you're going to try something *anyway*, you are better off anticipating success.

For the fact is this: *other things being equal, those who believe in and visualize the positive are more likely to achieve it.* I once read an article about a teacher who started the school year with a new group of students. The principal, as part of his own experiment, chose students' names at random and then divided them into two lists. The first group, according to what the principal told the teacher, consisted of well-behaved A-grade students; the other group comprised students who were more difficult to handle and not as academically successful. In fact, all of the students were about equal in their behaviour and potential for academic achievement. However, as a result of the teacher's expectations and the way in which she subsequently dealt with each of the students, the group of "A students" did in fact live up to the teacher's expectations. They all performed better academically and complied with classroom rules. The other group was less successful in the classroom—both behaviourally and academically.

Why? My educated guess is that the kids in the first group were injected with optimism: their behaviour was part of a self-fulfilling prophecy. When parents or teachers expect children to behave poorly, label them as lazy or irresponsible, the children will develop commensurate expectations. The story illustrates not only the power of optimism, but the power of adults to instil it in kids.

When children are learning a new skill—swimming, for instance—their success in mastering strokes, breathing, diving, and tasks of endurance depends to a great extent on how they rate their chances of doing well. A very strong swimmer may present as weaker if he tells himself, "I can't make it across the whole length of the pool without stopping" or "I'll never be able to dive like my brother."

Optimism's best allies are preparation and hard work. When you know you've laid the ground for a great performance, it's much easier to step on stage with confidence. The greatest athletes do an enormous amount of training and practising: that is what gives them the "winning edge." So how does a parent move a child from lacking in confidence and ambition to feeling better about him- or herself and his or her future? Encouragement is key, but encouragement needs to focus on effort, improvement over time, and achieving the level *you* are capable of. So, instead of waiting for your child to be better than everyone else, use encouraging words to help him or her see that his or her hard work has allowed steady progress towards his or her own personal best.

I used to share a story with parents during my workshop *How to motivate your child for success: at home and in school.* It concerned a little boy who was very unmotivated about working on his handwriting skills. The parents received discouraging reports from his teacher about how he was not living up to his potential. They tried everything from threatening him to coaching him as he wrote lines of letters. Unfortunately, most of what the child heard were comments like "Your letters are too small," "You need to print neater," and "The way that you're holding the pencil is not right." After consulting with me on ways to motivate their son, they began giving attention to what they *liked.* When they next sat down with him, they focused on a round **o**. "Wow," the mother exclaimed, "look at that perfectly round **o.** It's a perfect circle. Your circles have really improved." The son's face lit up with the sense that this writing thing could actually go well. She continued with "Did you know that if you remove a little part of the **o** it can become a **c** and that if you draw a line to the right and up, it can become a **d**, or with a line to the left and down, it can become a **p**?" With his new vision of success, the child continued to create beautifully formed letters on every line. When he proudly presented his paper to his teacher the following day, she was astonished.

It's also important that we display optimism in our own behaviour, as a model for our children. When we're undertaking something that can reasonably be expected to succeed, we need to avoid making self-deprecating comments or dire predictions of disaster. Even when the odds are not as good, once we've committed to a certain course of action, our children need to see us using a positive attitude to stoke ourselves up.

The final twist about optimism is that it helps us fill in the winning strategy: it stimulates our imagination so we can see more clearly *how* to succeed, and that gives us an advantage over someone whose vision is clouded by gloom. Optimism actually promotes creativity.

It's easier to find a path through a maze when you believe there is one. And we can help our kids believe too.

The activity that follows will take approximately 15 minutes to complete. By the end of this activity, family members will realize that thoughts affect performance and that a positive or optimistic outlook can create more favourable results.

Dynamix Family Activity

Enacting Optimism

Activity name:

Penny for Your Thoughts!

Materials needed:

- Pennies
- Jars/bottles with various sized openings, the largest being at least four inches in diameter

Set-up:

Place a jar on the floor. Start with the jar that has the largest opening.

Directions:

Family members should take turns trying to drop a penny into the jar from a standing position. Before attempting the feat, each family member should think about how optimistic they are about the penny landing in the jar, and then share that with the group. If he or she is successful, he or she may try another jar with a smaller opening. As the activity proceeds, keep track of whether an optimistic/pessimistic attitude affected the person's ability to drop the penny into the jar. You will likely find that there is a correlation between attitude and result.

Even if at first you don't succeed, remain optimistic that practice makes perfect.

Discussion:

- Before you tried dropping your penny, did you think you were going to be able to get it into the jar? Why?
- Do you feel that these thoughts helped you or hurt you?
- Why do you think it is important to have a positive attitude?
- What helps you have a more positive attitude?
- When else is it important to have a positive attitude?

Chapter 19

Focus on Perseverance

"It's not that I'm so smart, it's just that I stay with problems longer."
—Albert Einstein

When people don't persevere, it is often because the early or mid-stages of a task make it seem endless, or impossible to excel at. When very little progress is evident, and the work is difficult, it is actually *hard to imagine* that by persisting, one can get to a place where things look different. But every time one pushes through to the surprise ending, it becomes less surprising. Persistence in one task makes the next task easier to stay with. So it is very important to give children the experience of finding out that the early discouraging signs are *misleading*; that if they soldier on, obstacles will melt away and the task will "submit" to them.

The following story illustrates all these points. A mother, Gloria, and her ten-year-old daughter, Jennifer, purchased a paint-by-number kit. Gloria was very excited because she had loved working on these kits as a child and was eager to share this activity with her daughter. However, when they sat down with paint brushes in hand and began reading the instructions, Gloria wondered if the process might be too challenging for her child. She kept this to herself and, once they got started, was actually impressed at how well her daughter was doing. It wasn't easy, though: Jennifer had to use just the tip of her brush to paint within the lines of tiny spaces and had to concentrate intensely for a long time in order to complete a single area. Then, about ten minutes into the activity, Jennifer looked up and compared her side of the canvas with her mother's. That was her downfall. "You're doing a much better job than me," the child said. "I'm doing a terrible job. I'm always going over the lines. And I'm way too slow. I'll never get my side done. I want to stop."

Gloria realized that along with the difficulty of the job she had added the issue of measuring up: Jennifer was comparing the quality and the speed of her own work to that of an accomplished adult, instead of enjoying her own skill level. So now she was defining "success" in a way that made it unachievable by her. But even without that factor, the truth was that the finish line looked unreachable to Jennifer, and she felt as if it would take forever to get even half done.

Gloria smiled at her daughter and said, "You know what? I think you're doing really well at this. When I first tried it, I was older than you and didn't do as well." Jennifer laughed and said, "For real?" Her mom said yes and then added, "You know what else? If you keep trying you'll not only get better at it but you'll get faster. But it's up to you. I've had fun and if you want to stop I'm fine with that."

Jennifer decided she wanted to try for "ten more minutes." After half an hour during which both were engrossed in their work, Gloria heard her daughter say, "Mom, look." She raised her head and found Jennifer beaming at her and pointing out a butterfly that was perfectly painted in green and gold. From then on, Jennifer couldn't be stopped. Her mom had to take a phone call and got caught up in other things, but for Jennifer, the playing field had not only been levelled but it had changed. What had felt like slogging through mud now felt like walking on firm grass. Jennifer had broken through the barrier of difficulty and found the place where steady improvement happens.

Over the following couple of weeks, she completed the whole canvas and others. More importantly, she had learned that the appearance of impossibility may be an *illusion*, hiding something that can be conquered. She had learned the surprise secret that only persistence can reveal.

There are many opportunities to foster perseverance. How about when your child says she would prefer to wear running shoes with Velcro straps because she doesn't want to bother learning to tie her shoelaces? Consider that although it may be easier on everyone to buy the Velcro variety, by doing so you are not encouraging your child to persevere with tasks that may be difficult at first. Velcro might be an option only after she has mastered tying her shoelaces. Consider how much perseverance (and patience) a child develops when fishing. Although it may be frustrating at first, if they persist, most children get the reward of being thrilled when the fish bite.

Other more challenging activities such as learning how to play the piano, play chess, or skate may require more patience on your end and more perseverance on theirs. Although children may want to quit soon after they've begun, encourage them to persevere through the more challenging initial stages so that they can learn the lesson that things get easier and the "impossible" becomes doable.

And consider how *you* model staying with a challenging activity. When modelling perseverance as an adult, it is important that your child sees you completing one task before moving onto the next. Or, in the case of multi-tasking, sees you taking each of your activities through to completion. If you regularly begin projects but don't end them, your child will tend to do the same.

When you are engaged in a challenging activity such as a crossword puzzle, does your child see you focused for longer, rather than brief, periods of time? Does she see you lost in thought, contemplating several options and alternatives before putting it aside? Does she see you asking others or researching answers to questions if you're not sure? This is all part of modelling perseverance.

Parents often rank persistence or perseverance extremely high on their list of attributes they hope to pass on to their children. However, we understandably discourage children from persevering when it comes to things like wanting another cookie or negotiating bedtime. In these situations, we say that our children are unrelenting or obstinate. Consider that persistence at these times—even when we don't want to give in to their whims or demands—is still perseverance. It may be wise to say something like "You are being incredibly persistent and that is great. However, there are times when you are going to be met with no. You may want to think of other ways to talk to me about solutions to your problem. Although you can't have another cookie right now, I am willing to talk about when you may have another." Or "You may be unhappy with your bedtime and frustrated that, despite your persistence, I am not budging. But I am willing to include you in making choices about other decisions that affect you."

The activity that follows will take approximately 30 minutes to complete. By the end of the activity, each player will be rewarded by recognizing that perseverance allows one to see successful results.

Dynamix Family Activity

Enacting Perseverance

Activity name:
Tangrams

Materials needed:

- Bristol board (or any paper will do)
- Scissors
- Perseverance

Set-up:
Go to www.getdynamix.com/characteristhekey and follow the instructions on how to build a Tangram set. Then print out the "Tangram shapes" page.

Directions:
The challenge is to work together or separately to reproduce the shapes from the "Tangram shapes" page by using the Tangram pieces. Make sure to abide by the following rules:

- All seven shapes must be used.
- There can be no holes or spaces between shapes.
- No shapes may overlap each other.

See "Tangram answers" at www.getdynamix.com/characteristhekey to see if you are correct. REMEMBER, this is about perseverance. The answer page is to let you know if you have put it together correctly, not to give you an easy route to the right answer. GOOD LUCK!

(*Continued*)

Discussion:

- At any point in the activity did you feel like giving up? If yes, when and why? How hard did the task look to you at that point?
- How did you encourage yourself to continue?
- How did you feel about yourself when you successfully completed the task? Did your earlier opinion of the task still seem valid?
- How do you think you might have felt if you hadn't persevered?

Chapter 20

Focus on Respect

"Respect for ourselves guides our morals; respect for others guides our manners."
—Laurence Sterne

There are several different meanings of "respect," and if we are to foster it in our children and model it for them, we need to separate the different strands and see which are more useful. Let's look at some of them.

It used to be said, "Always respect your parents," meaning *do exactly as they tell you*. But respect is in fact not the same thing as obedience. Nor is it automatically our right just because we are parents. Respect should be earned.

Sometimes, parents confuse strong will or "a mind of his own" with disrespect. A parent recently told me that she found her seven-year-old child extremely disrespectful when he resisted their attempts at getting him to change out of his pyjamas and into his clothes. She felt that he was being disrespectful in not complying with their request (ultimately their demand), and more so by screaming and shouting when he was physically made to change into his clothes.

In fact, the child's response was to be expected. No one likes to be told what to do and then forced, against their will, to do what they have stated they will not. Children are not soldiers. They don't always respond to orders with compliance. It takes understanding and strength on the part of a parent to be able to stand back from this kind of reaction so as not to take it personally. Then the parent may consider why else the child may be challenging the request. By understanding where the child is coming from, a parent may see beyond the accusation of disrespect.

To get to this place, parents need to first examine their style of parenting. What I mean by this is that if you take the stance of an authoritarian parent, you most likely will consider any lack of compliance a form of disrespect. However, if you believe in a more democratic style of parenting and believe that children should be treated as social equals (which means that they are entitled to the same consideration as you when it comes to what is expected of them), then you may be more inclined to consider their thoughts and feelings when asked to do something. For example, if a father and daughter are relaxing together and the father says, "Get me a drink of water," would you say that the child should jump up from whatever she is doing and run to get it (assuming Dad is not coughing and needing the water right away)? If you have a more democratic viewpoint, you would respect the child's rights too and recognize that as a social equal, she has the right, for example, to ask her father to wait a few minutes until she has finished what she is in the middle of doing. If we model respect for our children as social equals, they will likely treat us with the same respect.

At this point, "respect" stops meaning obedience in the sense of the traditional "minding your elders" and takes on the more valid meaning of *showing regard for another person*. Obedience has the drawback that it is unilateral; if you order your kids around, you are not modelling something that you would want them to do to you. (But that is exactly what you are likely to get back from them, or see them doing to each other!) Real respect means acknowledging the dignity and value of other persons, and spreads to other living things and the planet as a whole. When you treat your kids in a way that doesn't insult their dignity, they are more likely to treat others, including you, that way too.

Being social equals does not mean, of course, that children make decisions reserved for adults. Decisions such as which house to buy or how late children can come home from a party may not be open for discussion. Recognizing that certain rules and guidelines are valid and sound, and ultimately for one's own benefit, is another part of respect. In order for there not to be chaos and anarchy, we all have to uphold rules that have been established in appropriate and rational ways.

As parents, we can model this kind of respect by adhering to rules that apply to us, even if we don't always like them. For example, even if you are frustrated by how long it is taking for a pedestrian light to grant you permission to cross the road, modelling patience and respect for this rule by waiting for the light to change colour is imperative if you want to lead by example.

The same point applies to wearing a seatbelt, for example. If we lead our children to believe that the only reason we are wearing one is so we won't get spotted by a policeman who will issue us a ticket for breaking the law, then we are teaching that we only comply through intimidation, not because we respect the fact that seatbelts keep everyone safer in case of an accident. Just as a curiosity, ask your children why we wear seatbelts. I have heard many say, "So that we don't get into trouble." If they do respond in this way, it may be helpful for them to learn why else rules should not be broken. If we frown on or show disrespect towards rules that have been established to create order, it may be difficult to encourage our children to follow guidelines that we have established at home. So long as the rules we create are fair, children should be willing to follow them.

To be fair to our children, it is important to honour their need to know why specific rules are created. In fact, if rules make sense, children are much more inclined to follow them. An educator shared a story about *his* grade 8 teacher who gave him a reasonable explanation as to why people should be polite and nice to one another. Up until that time, he thought of being polite as part of a whole bunch of rules he didn't particularly want in his life. When his teacher explained that the reason for being polite wasn't just about following rules—shared that there was a reward for being polite to others—that it made the mannerly person and the person on the receiving end *feel good*—this made all the difference. The child understood what the benefits to being polite were (to himself and others) and no longer felt that he had to be polite just because he was being told to behave that way. Manners are themselves a part of respect—part of *showing regard for others*. And this educator's story suggests what the "life lesson" is that respect carries with it. We feel good when we treat others with respect, and when we are treated that way by them. That good feeling, I think, springs from the sense that all beings, including ourselves, have innate dignity. That's a wonderful, uplifting thing to know. When children see respect being modelled, receive it from their parents, and learn to practise it, that inspiring truth will dawn on them.

Let's talk about some good ways to model and teach respect.

My friend Barb, a mother of three, told me about one technique that works well. When members of her family are rude or disrespectful to one another, she models patience and fairness by giving them a chance to reverse and start over. For example, suppose they sit down at the dinner table and one of her children uses a disrespectful tone of voice accompanied with words such as "I didn't want milk. Who poured milk in my glass?" Barb will remain calm and say, "Please reverse. Go back upstairs, then come down and start over." This usually does the trick. So long as she remains calm and non-punitive, the children usually do as asked. What's important, she says, is to be open to reversing as a parent too. A few days prior to our discussion, Barb said that when *she* came out to the car in a grumpy mood, her seven-year-old son asked her to go back inside, come back, and start over. She did as requested and, after a moment of silent reflection in the house, returned to the car in a very different frame of mind.

There are so many other wonderful, yet simple, ways to model respect. Have you ever thought about what a great role model you are when you take your empty containers out of a movie theatre and dispose of them? Not only are you modelling respect towards the people who clean the theatre but also towards the environment by disposing of the garbage in the proper recycling containers. Even a gesture as simple as putting your shopping buggy back in the corral goes a long way towards modelling respect. Then, when you ask your children to put the scissors or glue back where they took them from, they will not see you as being hypocritical. Other simple gestures include holding the door open for another person to enter, letting another driver pull his car in front of yours in a long line of traffic, holding an elevator open a few seconds longer for another passenger, arriving for an appointment as scheduled, and offering your seat to an older or disabled person.

Another way in which we model respect is by not discriminating against others who are born to a family with a religious, ethnic, or cultural background other than our own or towards others because of their sexual preference or lifestyle. It's so easy to casually undermine, mock, or talk in generalities about people who are "different." Children are tuned in to everything that they hear. If we speak in a demeaning way about other cultures or lifestyles, children grow up intolerant of differences rather than embracing them and wanting to learn more about them.

In addition to modelling respect towards others—our children, our partners, family, friends, neighbours, and strangers—it is important that we consider how we model respect for ourselves.

When you say something like "I'm such an idiot, I should have known better" or "I never look good in anything I wear," your children hear self-loathing and may mimic you when talking about themselves. They may say something like "I never understand the math at school. I'm stupid" or "I hate the way I look." Instead of modelling a lack of self-respect, how about saying something like "I'll remember to do that differently next time" or "This outfit no longer suits me but I'm sure I can find something else that does look good." Although it may be more difficult to come up with words that honour rather than deflate yourself, consider the impact that your words are having on your children.

Part of modelling self-respect, I realize, is modelling healthy eating and exercise. However, my day, like yours, is filled with so much else that even 30 minutes for the treadmill seem hard to find. After numerous attempts on my teenage daughter's part to get me back on the treadmill, I put her to the test. After she had rhymed off a list of what she needed help with that evening, I told her that I'd be happy to help—after I'd been on the treadmill. She passed the test with flying colours. She backed right off and said she would wait. Our children occasionally like to see us putting ourselves first!

The activity that follows will take approximately 15 to 20 minutes to complete. During it, family members are asked to take part in an extremely frustrating exercise. By the end of the activity, everyone will have an opportunity to discuss how they felt they were treated by the others during the exercise and at other times.

Dynamix Family Activity

Enacting Respect

Activity name:

Take It Back

Materials needed:

- One tube of toothpaste (can be travel-size)
- One paper plate
- Toothpicks
- Q-tips
- A voice recorder (optional)

Set-up:

Place the tube of toothpaste on the plate and remove the cap. Place a toothpick and Q-tip for each member of your family on the plate beside the tube of toothpaste.

(Optional) Place a voice recorder somewhere in the room to record what your family says during this activity.

Directions:

With everyone sitting together around the plate, tell your family that you will completely empty out the tube of toothpaste onto the centre of the plate. Once that is done, explain to them that you are all now, as a team, going to try to refill the tube of toothpaste using only the toothpicks and Q-tips you have been given. Explain that the goal is to do this in less than five minutes. Have fun with it, but be sure to take mental notes on the way everyone treats each other as you attempt to accomplish

(*Continued*)

a very frustrating task. Not surprisingly, it is extremely difficult or impossible to refill the tube of toothpaste with these materials.

After a five-minute time limit, have everyone put their toothpicks and Q-tips down. Use this activity as an opportunity to reflect on how everyone treats each other.

Discussion:

- Did we treat each other the way we like to be treated?
- Can anyone think of a time when they were treated with respect? How did it feel? With disrespect? How did you feel then?

Another interesting point of discussion would be to highlight the similarities between the toothpaste and our words and actions. Sometimes we may say or do things that we would like to take back but, just like the toothpaste, once our words or actions are out, they are extremely difficult to retract!

(Optional) Play back your conversation from the voice recorder and discuss when and how family members showed respect and disrespect.

Chapter 21

Focus on Responsibility

"If you want children to keep their feet on the ground,
put some responsibility on their shoulders."
—Abigail Van Buren

Most parents place "responsibility" high on the list of what they want to see from their children. At school, children are expected to be responsible for ensuring that they have taken home all that they need to complete their homework assignments. At home, parents often expect their children to take on certain household responsibilities, often referred to as "chores."

One of the most common questions I get from parents is how to motivate their children to become more responsible. It's no secret that most children would do anything to get out of having to help with dishes, laundry, and making beds. Even the most industrious, responsible parents have a difficult time influencing their children to engage in what is perceived as monotonous, boring labour. So I don't want to guarantee you that even if you are the most responsible parent in the world, your children will follow in your footsteps when it comes to household responsibilities.

However, consider this question: when children shirk their "responsibilities," are they perhaps rebelling against being *told* what to do? Is the delegation of chores democratic? The best way to maintain a co-operative working team and to help each family member feel personally responsible is to discuss the household chores and who should be responsible for what—based on various factors including age, availability, and ability. Some family members may prefer to adopt a chore on a permanent basis and others may like variety. In the case of a family member who prefers change, a rotating schedule can be discussed. In other words, children (and adults) are more likely to want to work together if they have been part of the planning stages.

In fostering a sense of responsibility, it's also important not to do someone else's work for them. A client told me that she wanted her 18-year-old son to take on more responsibility. She told him that he should sponsor a child in another country, and got him the information about how to go about the process. She then offered to help him out financially if he wasn't able to come up with the amount he agreed upon every month. I couldn't help but mention that even if her son were to take on this "responsibility," it would likely be short-lived. In order for him to become a responsible person, he would first need to *want* to take on this commitment. In her attempt to encourage responsibility, she was instead taking more responsibility on herself! Fearful that he would never be capable of living on his own and taking care of himself, she didn't know what else to do.

I suggested that she begin closer to home. Knowing that she often rescued her son from failing, and keeping in mind the previous point about democratic allocation of tasks, I suggested that they have a discussion about the fair division of chores and responsibilities around the house, and of the consequences (not punishments) if one person didn't hold up their end. (For example, one mom negotiated this logical consequence with her son who repeatedly forgot to bring his hamper to the laundry room: they decided that if the dirty clothes weren't in the laundry room by Sunday evening, he would have to wash and fold his own clothes once she had completed her laundry duties for the rest of the family.)

From our discussion, my client also learned that even though she had modelled responsibility by maintaining and organizing the household, she possibly had done too good a job. By thinking it was her responsibility to always hold her son's hand and catch him when he fell, she did not allow him to see his own responsibilities through. Once she recognized this, she was able to step back and allow him to grow as a responsible adult.

Children today often want (and need) more responsibility than they are given. An 18-year-old client shared with me that the most compelling reason to attend university away from his hometown was to prove his capabilities to his parents. He felt that he could do more than what they thought he was capable of. He wanted to take the garbage to the curb each week, take care of his own laundry, and deal with the consequences if he didn't get his homework done on time.

What we have been discussing is being "responsible" in the sense of being faithful to a task or commitment. When children get used to carrying out their commitments and seeing their obligations through, they notice a new and gratifying thing: others (especially adults) increasingly rely on them. It feels good to be needed and trusted, so responsibility breeds a sense of being part of a team, whose greater good is above one's own interests. When the coach asks you to put the equipment away because he knows you will do it right, or your dad asks you to stay with your tired sister while he runs to the drug store for cough drops, you get a sense that you are seen as someone who won't blow a crucial task on which others' welfare depends. As we mature, we realize that a wider group depends on us to do our part: we are not just responsible *for* various tasks, but are responsible *to* the people who depend on us. (That is why team sports provide such great training in responsibility.) The feeling of being seen as reliable makes one glad to take on responsibilities and to deliver on them. Eventually it offers up an even greater gift: a joy in providing service to others.

The word "responsible" has a separate meaning which is also part of the virtue in question. That is to "own" our own actions and their consequences, to admit what we have caused. So another way in which we can model the trait is by "admitting responsibility" for our words and actions when they cause harm. As parents it's often not easy to humble ourselves by admitting we were wrong—that our words or actions were not the best—and then by apologizing. If our children respectfully point out where we have gone wrong, we model responsibility by listening to what they are saying and then agreeing with them, even when our instinct is to become defensive and to retaliate emotionally.

Most of us are more conscious about admitting responsibility when our children are around us. But how about when you're on your own? Let's say, for example, that you scrape a car as you're backing out of a parking spot. Do you leave a note or leave the scene? When professional speaker and author Dr. Mike Thomson and I talked about this scenario, he said that how parents behave when the kids aren't in the car is "the true acid test." During his presentations to parents, he uses a neat device that he calls "the newspaper test." This test requires that a parent, prior to choosing a certain action in life (such as whether leaving after scraping the parked car), ask themselves whether or not they would want their sons and daughters to read an article about the incident and what he or she did—on the front page of a newspaper. If the parent would rather his or her children not read the article, it is of course a sign that it's a poor choice. The potency of the newspaper test shows that we want the character we show our kids to be real, by reflecting the person we are *all the time*. Each of us wants to be a person worthy of the role of parent—worthy of having a kid point to us with pride and say, "That's my dad" or "That's my mom."

The activity that follows may take up to an hour depending on the complexity of the recipe you choose in the family bake-a-thon. By the end of the activity, each person will be more aware of how important it is for everyone to assume their responsibilities seriously if their recipe is to be a success.

Dynamix Family Activity

Enacting Responsibility

Activity name:

Family Bake-a-thon

Materials needed:

- A favourite baking recipe and the ingredients required. You may go to www.getdynamix.com/characteristhekey for a few recipe ideas or pick your own.

Set-up:

Make sure that you have all the ingredients in your kitchen.

Directions:

Almost every child loves to bake with the family. Baking is a great way to work on a project together. Sit down with the family before you begin this activity and ask each member to take on specific responsibilities. Depending on your children's ages, one child might request or be assigned the responsibility of collecting all the ingredients from around the kitchen, another may be responsible

(*Continued*)

for collecting all of the utensils and pans needed, and another may be responsible for weighing and measuring. And guess who will likely be responsible for the clean-up! Try to encourage your children to work with you during clean-up. Young children love to help wash dishes in warm, soapy water and older children can help with drying or putting dishes away. When your creation is ready, sit down to enjoy it together. While eating, you can discuss the activity.

Discussion:

It is critical that you positively reinforce your children's efforts. Giving positive reinforcement to children after seeing them take care of their responsibilities makes it more likely that they will repeat these behaviours in the future.

When giving positive reinforcement, make sure that you are specific and reinforce their choice. So, don't just say, "Great job, Carrie!" Instead say, "Great Job, Carrie! I love how carefully you put the dishes away."

While this experience will speak for itself, here are some discussion points and questions you can ask your children:

- Did everyone have fun?
- How does it help to have everyone share in the responsibilities?
- Do you think it is easier for one person to do all the work or for everyone to be responsible for a little bit of the work? Why?
- Would you like to bake something as a family again?

Conclusion

As parents, you certainly understand the meaning of responsibility. However, you may have been surprised by how many other important characteristics there were to model. And the list doesn't stop with the ten I featured or even with the others you have added to the plan. You'll continue to think of other attributes to model and instil in your children. Characteristics such as a sense of humour, patience, tolerance, flexibility, resiliency, and loyalty are some that I have added to my personal list.

Now that you know what it means to model character on an ongoing basis, I hope the challenge to influence your kids for good no longer feels as daunting as it may have at the start. By following The Family Plan and continuing to meet monthly, you and your family will get to the point where living a life of character is second nature to you. So take it slow and steady. Be as patient with yourself as you try to be with your children.

I don't want to mislead you by saying that modelling good character is a magic wand that you can wave to create perfect little people, so that your kids will compete with each other to set the table first, get up the earliest every morning, and be the first to comply with every request you make. However, I can assure you that over time, as you continue to model character, you will see positive changes in your children and in the way family members interact with one another. Character truly is the key to unlocking the best in our children—and ourselves.

As American educator Dr. Howard Kirschenbaum* says, "I have seen many young people grow up in homes where the parents are steadily modelling and teaching and the kids turn out to be fine young people who are not only enjoying life themselves but are making positive contributions in the world. It gives one a sense of optimism and faith that the beliefs we have about raising young people really work. Character education makes for cohesive families across generations."[1]

Join me in working towards creating a new "normal." A normal where living with character is considered the accepted standard of behaviour.

We have come full circle. I wrote at the very beginning of this book that we have no choice but to intentionally model character to our kids if we want them to have good values. Who else will our children learn from if not us?

If your children grow up wanting to be good people, if they truly believe in following their conscience rather than the crowd, an amazing thing will happen. They will draw really good people to them. They will find that the friends who are attracted to them will be loyal and genuine—the kind of people who will not gossip behind their backs or lead them down a destructive path. Sometimes, the journey towards becoming a good person can be a little lonely. In a society that seems to feel that it's cool to break rules, your child may feel that he or she stands alone in wanting to be a person of good character. That's why a strong connection to family and solid reinforcement of character attributes are so

* Author Howard Kirschenbaum, Ed.D., is Professor Emeritus, Warner Graduate School of Education and Human Development, University of Rochester in New York.

important. With them, your children will grow towards achieving their full potential.

Thank you for joining me on this journey. Before I close, I invite you to consider what you have accomplished and learned:

1. Your family has built a framework within which to define your core values and beliefs. You have begun to model good character for your children, and have found many ways to encourage good character in them.
2. You have developed a common language in defining the top ten character traits—all keys to your success as a family.
3. You have developed skills that allow each family member to observe and analyze his or her own behaviour and behaviours of others within the family and the community.
4. You have examined how the family as a whole, as well as each individual member's behaviour, has an impact on each other, the community and globally.
5. You most likely feel part of a more connected, cohesive unit. You feel that your family's foundation is more solid and secure and that you can trust each other and communicate openly and honestly—without fear of being judged or ridiculed.
6. You have established future goals for each family member and for the group as a whole. By doing this, individual members and the family can strive for increased self-awareness and positive changes in behaviour.

Anne Frank, famous for the diary that she kept while in hiding during the Holocaust, wrote (in regard to children), "Parents can only give good advice or put them on the right paths, but the final forming of a person's character lies in their own hands." The future, too, lies in the hands of the children we are raising today. Therefore a lot depends on putting them on that right path. I feel a sense of optimism as I see younger children developing a new language of values and incorporating it into their lives. There is something magical about this opportunity for children to move our future in a positive direction.

Schools are helping children develop good character every day. By reading this book and deciding to add the crucial contribution that only parents can make, you are giving your child the key to lifelong success. You are also contributing to making this an improved world, in which people treat each other better and work together for the good of all.

I believe that our children will help us find the will to show them the right way. As our journey together comes to an end, so yours is just beginning. As you turn the last pages of this book, take time to embrace your children and to thank them for encouraging you, just by their very existence, to become the best person you can be.

Acknowledgments

I have always cautioned parents about using the word "good" in reference to their children's behaviour. Instead of "good girl," I've suggested statements such as, "Thanks for helping me load the dishwasher. It made my job much easier." However, I feel quite okay with the word "good" in this book's title. We all want our children to be good—knowing right from wrong and caring for others. We also want to raise our children to be good people as they grow into adults. In this book, the word "good" also has another meaning. Influencing our children "for good" means looking to the future and anticipating our children's goodness spilling over into generations yet to come.

Along the way to becoming a "good" person, I have had many wonderful mentors and role models.

My parents, especially, modelled the characteristics consistent with being people of good character. My mother modelled respect, honesty and doing unto others as you would have done unto you. My father modelled responsibility, initiative and empathy.

As a result of writing this book, my life has been enriched by many other exceptional people. When the book was first published in 2009 by Wiley & Sons, it was titled *Character Is the*

Key. While writing it, I had the opportunity to learn from leaders in the field of character education and to connect with some very special families who opened themselves up to the possibility of learning and growing.

I also had the good fortune to meet and talk to so many others—amazing teachers, principals, counsellors, writers and philanthropists who inspired me with their passion and commitment and honoured me with their time and honest sharing.

Part of what makes this book unique is that it provides exercises and opportunities for parents and their children to work together in enacting character traits and learn through experiencing them. I could not have done this without the help of Mitch Zeltzer, Corey Szwarcok and Adam Kertesz, the original co-founders of Dynamix. These dynamic young men, who developed the exercises at the end of each of the chapters in Part Three of the book, helped bring the character traits to life. I truly appreciate their support.

I'd like to extend a million thanks to the seven families (plus my own) who worked with me in trying on The Family Plan for size. If not for their support, enthusiasm, commitment and work, I would not have known what worked in "real" life. To my clients—thank you for giving me permission to base some of the stories in this book on your lives. As promised, your names and other identifying information have been changed to protect your privacy. And thanks to my dear friends and family who have offered advice, encouragement and support along the way.

To "Nini"—a darling childhood friend who now lives in Australia—thanks for allowing me to include the beautiful poem you wrote and recited to your parents on your wedding day.

After five years of supporting me and *Character Is the Key*, Wiley & Sons sold my book (along with others) to HarperCollins and so has begun what I know will be a wonderful relationship. Editorial Director Brad Wilson was open to my idea of changing the name of this book to *How to Influence Your Kids for Good* so as to help parents understand the intention behind writing it. Thanks to Brad and the rest of the HarperCollins team for supporting me and for allowing me to breathe new life into the book.

And last, but definitely not least, thanks to my devoted husband, Joey. I am grateful to have you working alongside me in modelling character to our children and for your support and encouragement every step of the way. To my amazing children—Talia and Chloe—you make me want to be the most intentional, most conscious and best parent I can be. Seeing you grow into the "good" people you are and observing you caring for one another, your family and others inspires me to continue believing in my ability to influence you by modelling with intention.

To everyone who is about to embark on this incredible journey, thank you for joining me. Your children will one day thank you too.

References

Introduction

1. When different cultures, creeds, and ethnic traditions are all represented in the student body, how does the school decide which of their rules and values should be taught? Thomas Lickona discusses this question in chapter 3 of his book, *Educating for Character*, (Bantam, 1991) and in his article "The Return of Character Education," *Educational Leadership*, 51(3), pp. 6–11, Nov. 1993.

2. For more information, read *Values Clarification: A Handbook of Practical Strategies for Teachers and Students*, by S. Simon, L. Howe, and H. Kirschenbaum, published by Hart, 1972.

3. In conversation with Dr. Marvin Berkowitz, 2008.

Chapter 1

1. In conversation with Kathleen Redmond, 2008.

2. T. Lickona, "Character Education, Relativism, and Moral Truth," paper presented at the conference "Beyond Relativism," George Washington University, Washington, D.C., May, 1999.

Chapter 5

1. M.W. Berkowitz and J. Grych, "Fostering Goodness: Teaching Parents to Facilitate Children's Moral Development." *Journal of Moral Education*, 27, 371–391.

2. "The Power of Modelling in Children's Character Development," by Thomas Lickona, in D. Streight (Ed.), *Parenting for Character: Five Experts, Five Practices*. Council for Spiritual and Ethical Education, 2008.

3. In conversation with Dr. Marvin Berkowitz, 2008.

Chapter 6

1. A Touchstone is a reference point against which other things can be evaluated. In 2005, the school's student leadership team composed a Touchstone for the school at which Birenbaum taught—following a process of consulting with students, staff, and parent representatives. Each day, one of the seven phrases from the Touchstone—such as *We embrace each other's differences and care for each other's feelings*—is read during morning announcements over their public address system. In addition, a mural featuring their Touchstone graces the front foyer of the school and teachers integrate the phrases into their teaching.

Chapter 7

1. Thomas Lickona, Introduction, *Character Matters: How to Help Our Children Develop Good Judgment, Integrity, and Other Essential Virtues* (New York: Touchstone, 2004).

2. *Character Education, Parents as Partners*, Educational Leadership, September, 2005, by Marvin W. Berkowitz and Melinda C. Bier.

3. For more information, read M. Schwartz, *The Modeling of Moral Character for Teachers: Behaviors, Characteristics, and Dispositions That May Be Taught. Journal of Research in Character Education*, 5(1), 2007, pp. 1–28, Information Age Publishing, Inc.

Chapter 8

1. "*Family Meetings*," pp. 145–146 in *Teaching Parenting the Positive Discipline Way*, Lynn Lott, M.A., M.F.T, and Jane Nelsen, Ed.D., M.F.T., 6th Edition Copyright 2008 by Lynn Lott and Jane Nelsen.

Chapter 15

1. *Am I a Normal Parent?* by Sara Dimerman (New York: Hatherleigh, 2008).

2. To read more: Thomas Lickona, *Character Education, Relativism, and Moral Truth*, paper presented at the conference "Beyond Relativism," George Washington University, Washington, D.C., May, 1999.

Chapter 17

1. *Character Education, Parents as Partners*, Educational Leadership, September, 2005, by Marvin W. Berkowitz and Melinda C. Bier.

Conclusion

1. In conversation with Dr. Howard Kirschenbaum, 2008.

Index

A

ADHD (Attention Deficit Hyperactivity Disorder), 74
Adler, Alfred, 97
All I Really Need To Know I Learned in Kindergarten (Fulghum), 79
Am I a Normal Parent? (Dimerman), 177
Anger, dealing with, 48, 56, 59, 60
Alcohol, 56
  and underage drinking, 27, 39, 47, 65
Autism, 157
Awards, for character, 10, 71, 74

B

Behaviour
  and consequences of, 44, 45, 49, 52, 53
  lessons from observation, 35–36, 39, 41, 59–60, 100, 106–7, 122–28, 179–80, 189, 229
  parent-child comparison, 29, 34, 43, 49, 153
  See also Parents, parenting; Teenagers; *and specific character traits*
Berla, Nancy, 80
Berkowitz, Marvin, 10, 59, 63, 80, 197
Bier, Melinda, 80, 197
Birenbaum, Arthur, 72, 85, 86, 87
Bullies, bullying, 47, 71, 73, 78, 109, 110, 112, 152, 159, 173, 197

C

CBC, 63, 182
Centre for Character Leadership, 30
"Character Education" (Berkowitz, Bier), 80

Character Matters (educational program), 8, 21, 69, 70
See also School(s)
Children
stages of development, 28, 37, 51, 52, 54, 55, 58
See also Discipline; Family; *and specific character traits*
College of Psychologists of Ontario, 7
Columbine (school tragedy), 8
Communications
and body language, 112
common language for, 77, 107, 229
and couples, 26, 34 (*see also* Parents, parenting)
as a family, 72, 93, 98, 99, 100, 107, 128, 134, 144, 229
and role models (TV), 38, 39.
See also Family; I-messages
Conflict, confrontation
avoiding, 23, 24
and divorce, 46, 63
and marital behaviour, 60, 67
resolving, 32, 46, 59, 60, 62, 98, 99, 137, 145
Consequences vs. behaviour, 44, 45, 49, 52, 53
Courage, 9, 22, 24, 28, 39, 43, 50, 57, 113, **116**, 126, **171**, 197
as character trait, 114, 117, 123
Dynamix exercise on, 174, 175
experiences related to, 152
and facing fear, 152, 171, 172, 173, 174, 175
and intergrity, 173
modelling of, 48, 52, 55, 173
See also Bullies, bullying

D

Dimerman, Chloe, 10, 73, 151
Dimerman, Talia, 95, 96 180, 181
Disabilities,
and empathy, 163, 164
Discipline, 43, 94–96
approach to, 52
and consequences of behaviour, 44, 45, 49, 52, 53.
See also No screens policy; Obedience
Divorce
impact on children, 56, 63, 64, 66, 67
and parenting, 64, 65, 66
statistics regarding, 63
Dreikurs, Rudolf, 97
Dynamix (organization), 13, 150
toolbox for family activities, 162–64, 168–69, 174–75, 184–87, 191–94, 198–99, 204–5, 211–12, 219–20, 225–26
See also specific character traits

E

Empathy, 9, 23, 24, 62, 70, 73, 88, **115**, 123, 125, 135, 136, 140, **155**
as character trait, 114, 117, 155, 157, 159
and charity work, 74–76, 119, 131, 156, 158
developing capacity for, 113, 156, 157, 158, 159, 161, 162
Dynamix exercise for, 162–64

and media, 159
modelling of, 48, 52, 54, 55, 58, 64, 74, 112, 142, 155, 157, 160, 161
Empowerment, 32, 138, 160, 168

F

Fairness, 9, 22, 23, 27, 28, 31, 38, 60, **116**, 125, 169, 197
childrens' view of, 137, 165, 167, 168
and discipline, 167
Dynamix exercise for, 168–69
and favoritism, 166, 167
modelling of, 23, 25, 26, 44, 45, 52–55, 64, 88, 166, 167, 168, 216
Family, families
communications, 31, 107, 119, 121, 137, 145
detachment from, 94, 139
diversity of, 133, 138, 217
and goal setting, 130–31
impact of family of origin, 24, 25, 26, 60
meetings, 29, 32, 57, 93, 96–99, 102, 104–132
as democratic process, 104, 144
incentives to participate, 105, 122
minutes of (recording), 112, 150
preparation for, 104, 106, 149
success of, 103, 131
timing of, 102, 117, 149
toolbox for, 108–9, 117–19, 120–21, 123–24, 127–28, 130–31 (*see also* Dynamix)
as moral foundation, 80, 84, 93, 94, 102, 132, 228
needs of, 23, 24, 34, 72, 104, 112, 113–15, 120
and touchstone, 72
See also specific character traits
Family Meetings (Lott), 97
Family Plan, The, 12, 17, 57, 60, 61, 64, 69, 89, 100, 101, 102, 103, 107, 111, 123, 139, 227
success of, 134, 135, 137, 140, 141, 142, 144, 145
Fassel, Kelly, 85
Fear, 171–75. *See also* Courage
Feinstein, Lana, 42, 159
Frank, Anne, 229
Free The Children (charity), 74–77
Fulghum, Robert, 79

G

Glaze, Avis, 8
Glendon College, 75
Grych, John, 59

H

Havercroft, John, 8
Henderson, Anne, 80
Hoffman, John, 54
Holocaust, 229
Honesty, 9, 22, 26–27, 64, 86, 109, 114, **115**, 117, 123–24, 135, 178–80
and children, 183
Dynamix exercise for, 184–87

Honesty (*cont*)
emotional, 97, 98
and lying, 177, 178, 181
modelling of, 25, 48, 178
and peers, 179, 180
rewards of, 180, 181
"Honesty is still the best policy" (Urban), 180
How to motivate your child for success: at home and in school (Dimerman, workshop), 203

I

"I-messages", 129, 142
Initiative, 9, 22, 24, 114, **116,** 117, 123, 125
Dynamix exercise for, 191–94
modelling of, 49, 70, 137, 189, 190
Integrity, 9, 22, 39, 113, 114, **116,** **195**, 197
challenges to, 196
Dynamix exercise for, 198–99
and loyalty, 196, 197
modelling of, 48, 55, 57, 109, 140, 189, 198.
See also Courage; Peer culture
It's All About Character (organization), 197

K

Kirschenbaum, Howard, 228

L

Leave Out Violence (organizaton), 159
Lickona, Thomas, 33, *33n,* 60, 80, 180
"Long Term Parenting" (worksheet), 42
Lott, Lynn, 97, 98
Lying, reasons for, 177, 178, 181. *See also* Honesty

M

Media, impact of, 10, 38, 39, 56, 158, 159. *See also* Violence
Modelling, 22, 24, 139, 228
and character formation, 4–6, 228
impact of family of origin on, 3, 4, 23, 24, 26, 31, 73, 77
with intention, 7, 21, 23, 29, 30, 32, 48, 100, 102, 137, 152, 153, 182, 228
process of, 17
unconscious, 6, 13, 143
See also Teachers; *and specific character traits*
Moral issues (morality), 33, 34, 37, 60, 80, 109, 161
examples of, 25–29.
See also Integrity
Motivation, 46, 39, 104, 142, 178, 186, 221, 203

N

No screens policy, 94–96. *See also* Discipline

O

Obedience, 43, 45, 213, 214. *See also* Discipline

Optimism, 9, 23, 33, 56, 65, **116**, **201**, 203
as character trait, 24, 25, 208, 224, 227, 123, 126, 228
Dynamix exercise for, 204–5
modelling of, 52, 141, 173, 204
and power of positive thinking, 103, 113, 202, 204, 205

P

Parent Education Resource Centre, 7
"Parenting Today for Tomorrow" (Feinstein), 42
Parents, parenting
and children's education (*see* Schools)
consensus between, 29, 25, 34, 61, 65, 66, 67
as couples, 15–16, 25, 26, 29, 34, 57, 59, 61, 62, 63, 64, 67, 80, 88, 89, 139
habits of, 46, 48
influence of family of origin on, 3, 4, 23, 24, 26, 77
style of, 44, 50, 214
See also Discipline; Divorce; Modelling; Schools; *and specific character traits*
Peer culture, 70, 71, 73, 74, 157, 179, 180
and group pressure, 2, 3, 39, 47, 52, 56, 63, 160, 167, 196
Perseverance, 9, 22, 24, 26, 51, 52, 95, 113, **116**, 117, 135, 150, 211
and barriers of difficulty, 209
Dynamix exercise for, 211–12
examples of, 126, 207, 208
modelling of, 48, 58, 209, 210
Phobia, 172. *See also* Fear
Praise, as encouragement, 70, 101, 121, 131, 139–40

R

Redmond, Kathleen, 30
Respect, 9, 22, 27, 64, 70, 73, 83, 95, **97**, 99, **115**, 123, 128, 159, 179, 197, **214**, **215**, 219
as character trait, 23, 24, 45, 195
as a couple, 26, 29, 60, 61, 64, 142, 143
and discrimination, 166, 217
Dynamix exercise for, 219–20
and family, 87, 100, 103, 109, 110–14, 119, 128, 135, 136–37, 142, 216
and media, 159
modelling of, 25, 26, 29, 36, 39, 43–45, 48, 52, 54, 55, 59, 62, 64, 85–86, 198, 215–18, 220
and obedience, 213, 214
self respect, 118, 181, 218
Responsibility, 9, 22, 24, 27, 44, 45, 70, **115**, 129, 202, 225, 226
and chores, 136–37, 221–23
as a couple, 26, 66, 69
Dynamix exercise for, 225–26
modelling of, 25, 31, 33, 46, 48, 51, 52, 55, 58, 65, 72, 114, 224

Responsibility (*cont*)
and motivation, 221, 224
"newspaper test", 224
school vs. home, 87, 88
and teamwork, 223

S

School(s)
character-based assemblies, 71, 82, 88, 89
integration of special needs children, 157
-parent partnerships, 58, 80, 81, 82, 83, 87, 88, 89, 132, 144
teacher-parent relationship, 82–83, 85, 87
and teaching of character, 8–9, 71, 80–81, 86, 89, 132, 136, 230
See also Character Matters; Teacher(s)
Schwartz, Merle, 81, 84
Self-evaluation, 21, 32, 179
Sibling rivalry, 5, 142, 166
Stealing, 25, 26. *See also* Discipline

T

Teacher(s), 39, 46, 57, 71, 74, 109, 157, 180, 202
and character education, 85–86, 88, 216
as character models, 84, 85, 86
impact of, 82, 84
-parent collaboration, 58, 69, 82, 83, 85, 87, 88, 89
-student feedback, 84
See also Modelling; School(s)
Teams, teambuilding, teamwork, 13, 25, 26, 57, 73, 77–78, 84, 88, 89, 93, 98, 100, 101, 111, 120, 121, 139, 150, 222, 224
Teenagers, 22, 23, 27, 57, 83, 134, 140
communicating with, 14–15
and integrity, 196
and rebellion, 55, 56, 58, 141
See also Peer culture
Thomson, Mike, 197, 224
Touchstone Project, 72
Trust, 37, 49, 71, 107, 110, 113, 115, 178, 183, 190, 196, 205, 229

U

Urban, Hal, 180

V

Values, 30, 120, 131, 152
and acceptance, 75, 103
and couples, 34, 35, 60, 64
decline in, 8
defining, 25, 34, 72, 107, 115–16, 134, 229
integration into life, 149, 150, 195, 230
modelling of, 80, 108, 198, 228
prioritizing, 23, 24, 25
sense of, 21, 29
and society, 105, 109
transmission of, 31, 79, 87, 89, 93, 97
See also specific character traits
Violence, 17, 36, 160

and *Leave Out Violence* (organization), 159
and life experiences, 159, 160
media and, 27, 37, 158, 159
and teaching, 37
Virtues. *See specific character traits*

W

Weiss, Eric, 74, 77
Weiss, Jesse, 76
Weiss, Jordana, 74–77
Weiss, Julie, 74, 76, 77
Wilson, Lynn, 83
Woodside High School, 180

Y

York Region District School Board, 8, 9
York University, 75